Instructor's Manual for Psychiatric-Mental Health Nursing: Adaptation and Growth

Second Edition

Barbara Schoen Johnson, Ph.D., R.N., C.S.

Instructor's Manual prepared by

Suzanne Doscher, M.S., R.N.
Associate Professor
Medical University of South Carolina
College of Nursing
Charleston, South Carolina

Jane L. Assey, M.N., R.N.
Associate Professor
Medical University of South Caroli:'a
College of Nursing
Charleston, South Carolina

J.B. Lippincott Company   Philadelphia
London   Mexico City   New York   St. Louis   São Paulo   Sydney

Editor: Nancy Mullins
Production: Editorial Services of New England, Inc.
Printer/Binder: R.R. Donnelley & Sons

ISBN 0-397-54767-6

6 5 4 3 2 1

Any procedure or practice described in this book should be applied by the health-care practitioner under appropriate supervision in accordance with professional standards of care used with regard to the unique circumstances that apply in each practice situation. Care has been taken to confirm the accuracy of information presented and to describe generally accepted practices. However, the authors, editors and publisher cannot accept any reponsibility for errors or omissions or for consequences from application of the information in this book and make no warranty, express or implied, with respect to the contents of the book.

Every effort has been made to ensure drug selection and dosages are in accordance with current recommendations and practice. Because of ongoing research, changes in government regulations and the constant flow of information on drug therapy, reactions and interactions, the reader is cautioned to check the package insert for each drug for indications, dosages, warnings and precautions, particularly if the drug is new or infrequently used.

Contents

Part Six: Special Topics in Psychiatric-Mental Health Nursing

Part Seven: Crisis

Part Eight: Community Care from Crisis to Long-Term Intervention

Part Nine: Mental Health Interventions with the Medical Patient

Part Ten: Professional Issues in Psychiatric-Mental Health Nursing

Part One

Foundations of Psychiatric-Mental Health Nursing

Chapter 1
Introduction To
Psychiatric-Mental Health Nursing

Introduction

Chapter 1 introduces the student to the experience of psychiatric-mental health nursing. Pertinent historical as well as contemporary issues that impact on the delivery of psychiatric nursing care are discussed. Mental health and mental illness are defined and explored.

The author acquaints the student with the concept of stress and its significance to human behavior. Physiological responses to stress are presented within the framework of the General Adaptation Syndrome. Specific ego-defense mechanisms are cited as psychological responses that serve to help the person defend against stress/anxiety.

Attention is given to the need for self-awareness within the context of psychiatric nursing. The impact of self on the nurse-patient relationship is introduced. Also, self-awareness as it relates to choices made when coping with personal job stress is examined.

In addition, Chapter 1 briefly describes the nursing process as a framework to use while delivering psychiatric nursing care. This framework serves as a dimension of the American Nurses' Association's *Standards of Psychiatric and Mental Health Nursing,* which are presented within the chapter.

At the conclusion of Chapter 1, the author summarizes the following major points:

1. Mental health and mental illness are imprecisely defined states.
2. Satisfaction with one's characteristics, abilities, and accomplishments, effective and satisfying interpersonal relationships, effective coping or adaptation to one's life events, and personal growth characterize mental health.
3. The stigma attached to mental illness or disorder may hamper an individual's willingness to seek treatment and the rehabilitation process.
4. Problems hindering the progress of mental health care today are cost of treatment, separation of clients from their support systems, lack of governmental support of community mental health centers, and unequal access to care.
5. Stress is the nonspecific response of the body to any demand made on it.
6. Stressors, or stress-producing factors, whether physical or psychological, pleasant or unpleasant, elicit the same biologic stress response.
7. The General Adaptation Syndrome evolves in three stages—alarm reaction, stage of resistance, and stage of exhaustion.
8. Coping mechanisms, such as denial, rationalization, regression, and fantasy, protect the individual from anxiety.
9. Roles of psychiatric-mental health nurses include advocate, communicator, role model, member of the health team, and nurse-therapist.

10. Self-awareness, self-exploration, and working through of feelings and reactions to disturbed behavior are necessary for nurses to intervene in therapeutic ways.
11. Job stress and burnout can be minimized through an early detection of symptoms of stress, regular attention to physical health and exercise, and involvement in non-nursing activities.
12. The nursing process—assessment, nursing diagnosis, planning, intervention, and evaluation—is a problem-solving approach by which nurses deliver care to clients.

Key Terms

Mental health
Mental illness
Stress
Distress

General Adaptation Syndrome
Coping mechanisms
Nursing process

Teaching Strategies

1. Assign students to define and discuss their personal definitions of mental health and mental illness. Have them include in the discussion their beliefs regarding the following: (a) what, if any, differences there are between relationships experienced by a person who is mentally healthy and a person who is mentally ill, and (b) what, if any, differences there are between the reality base, the thought process, the affect, and the behavior of a person who is mentally healthy and a person who is mentally ill.
2. Encourage students to think about and share what they would think about and how they would feel about a neighbor, fellow student, or family member who had received inpatient or outpatient psychiatric care. How might they deal with their thoughts and feelings? How might this knowledge impact on their behavior?
3. Assign students to explore and identify mental health resources available within their community and the role of nurses within these resources.
4. Have students keep and submit to the instructor a diary with entries from each clinical contact. The diary is directed to be an introspective account of the student's thoughts, feelings, and reactions experienced in the clinical area. (This activity would receive no grade but would rather be used as a mechanism to encourage openness and honest introspection by the student.)
5. Encourage students to share their awareness of typical ways in which they deal with stress/anxiety, both physiologically and psychologically. Have students specifically identify and discuss their most frequently used coping mechanisms.

Supportive Materials

Cohen J, Struening EL: Opinions about mental illness scale. J. Abnorm Psychol 64:349–360, 1962
Doona ME (ed): Travelbee's Intervention in Psychiatric Nursing, pp 3–31. Philadelphia, FA Davis, 1979
Lego S: The one to one nurse-patient relationship. Perspect Psychiatric Care 18:67–72, 1980
Peplau HE: Some reflections on earlier days in psychiatric nursing. J Psychosoc Nurs Ment Health Serv 20:17–24, 1982

Chapter 2
Conceptual Frameworks
for Care

Introduction

Chapter 2 introduces the student to the four basic theories used by psychiatric-mental health nurses: psychoanalytic, behaviorist, biologic, and systems. The author's intent is to guide the understanding and behavior of nurses when these theories apply to real nursing situations.

The basic assumptions and tenets of each theory are explored, as well as the therapeutic approaches used in each. In addition, there is discussion of the application of each theoretical perspective to the practice of psychiatric-mental health nursing.

At the conclusion of Chapter 2, the author summarizes the following major points:

1. Psychoanalytic, behavioristic, and biologic theoretical perspectives emphasize that human behavior is largely determined by external forces or other factors outside the person's control; that is, the human being is viewed as a passive organism.
2. Systems theory acknowledges the effects of external forces on human behavior, but maintains that the individual can either influence these outside forces or can compensate for them; that is, the individual is viewed as an active and interactive human system.
3. Psychoanalytic, behavioristic, and biologic theoretical perspectives hold that human behavior is monocausal; in other words, human behavior is determined by one cause.
4. According to psychoanalytic theory, behavior is determined by early life events with parental figures.
5. Behavioristic theory holds that exposures to given stimuli and reinforcements determine how the human being learns to behave.
6. The biologic theoretical perspective holds that human behavior is determined by the individual's genetic and biologic makeup.
7. Systems theory asserts that human behavior has multiple causes.
8. All four theoretical perspectives are useful to nurses in assessing, diagnosing, planning, implementing, and evaluating nursing care.

Key Terms

Theory	Id
Libido	Superego
Pleasure principle	Ego

Sublimation
Reality principle
Unconscious
Psychosexual stages
Psychoanalysis
Token reinforcement
Shaping

Conscious
Preconscious
Input
Throughput
Output
Feedback

Teaching Strategies

1. Give verbal examples in class and have students identify the operative structure as id, ego, or superego. Example: Even though I really want to go to the football game, I should go to my cousin's birthday (superego).
2. Have students discuss, using examples, the relationship between the coping mechanisms and the ego-defense mechanisms.
3. Invite a guest speaker who practices a behaviorist approach. Examples: Weight-reduction program, token economy program with retarded citizens.
4. Discuss and differentiate between the application of systems theory to psychiatric patients and medical-surgical patients.
5. Encourage students to think of situations in their own lives in which they have used these theories instinctively.
6. Have students suggest different patient diagnoses, situations, and age groups in which one theoretical approach may be more helpful than another.
7. Create a debatelike situation in which each theory is argued pro and con by students.
8. Require a written, verbatim section of nurse (student)/patient interaction, and ask that a written analysis be performed using one of the theoretical frameworks.

Chapter 3
Nursing Theory and Psychiatric-Mental Health Practice

Introduction

Chapter 3 presents an overview and analysis of the concept of theory. The tentative nature of theory is emphasized, as is the function that theory serves in organizing, validating, and extending knowledge. The deductive, inductive, and analogic types of theory are defined.

The relationship between nursing theory development and the advancement of nursing as a discipline is highlighted. The theoretical works of Peplau, Orem, and Rogers are offered as examples of contributions that have helped advance nursing as a scholarly discipline. An analysis of the aforementioned theorists' works is presented. The analysis focuses on the classification of the particular theory, that is, interpersonal, behavioral, or analogic, and the function of the theory. The applicability of these theories to psychiatric-mental health nursing is discussed.

At the conclusion of Chapter 3, the author summarizes the following major points:

1. A theory is a conceptual system consisting of interrelated propositions that describe, explain, and predict selected phenomena.
2. All theories are tentative by nature and subject to change or to obsolescence.
3. The extent to which a theory is verified by scientific research determines its validity and usefulness.
4. A theory is not absolutely true.
5. A theory can usually be classified as deductive, inductive, or analogic in nature.
6. A theory functions to organize knowledge and to suggest ways of validating and extending knowledge through scientific research.
7. A theory also permits prediction of future events and thus serves as a guide to human action.
8. The development of theory is necessary for the development of nursing as a profession.
9. Most current nursing theories can be classified as interpersonal, behavioral, or systems-oriented in nature.
10. Hildegard Peplau, Dorothea Orem, and Martha Rogers, all of whom are pioneers in nursing theory development, have formulated theories applicable to psychiatric-mental health nursing.

Key Terms

Theory

Types of theory:

    Deductive

    Inductive

    Analogic

Types of nursing theories:

    Interpersonal

    Behavioral

    Systems-oriented

Teaching Strategies

1. Have students define in their own words the term *theory*. Compare and contrast individual definitions with the definition offered in Chapter 3.
2. Have students discuss their thoughts relative to the following statement made by the author of Chapter 3: "The development of theory, rather than the standardization of roles and procedures, is necessary for the further development of nursing as a profession."
3. Have students obtain from the psychiatric nursing literature one or more published articles that address the theories of Peplau, Orem, or Rogers. Have students orally present a synopsis of the article and critique the article's applicability to psychiatric-mental health nursing practice.
4. Have students compare and contrast the characteristics of the interpersonal, behavioral, and systems-oriented nursing theories.

Chapter 4
Communication

Introduction

Chapter 4 focuses on communication as an interpersonal process that is an indispensable component of psychiatric-mental health nursing. Emphasis is placed on assisting the student to understand and use the entire communication process. The goal of such efforts becomes that of developing with patients relationships that are helpful to both their understanding and learning more adaptive ways of dealing with their environment, as well as those adaptations that are professionally functional for the student nurse.

The communication process, including a specific nursing communication model, is discussed in detail. Communication assessment tools to identify and diagnose patient information and needs are suggested. Verbal and nonverbal communication techniques are discussed and described, using patient examples, highlighting key concepts, and pointing out specific barriers to communication. Guidelines for interviewing are mentioned. A sample process recording, applying therapeutic communication techniques, is included at the end of the chapter.

At the conclusion of Chapter 4, the author summarizes the following major points:

1. The purpose of communication is to give the patient a sense of identity and being.
2. Both verbal and nonverbal communication include three essential aspects: the transmission of information, the meaning of the transmission, and the behavioral effects of the transmission.
3. The Wenburg and Wilmot process model of communication is useful for nursing application because it emphasizes the behavioral aspects of the communication process and the variables that influence the process.
4. The components of the communication process are the sender, receiver, message, message variables, noise, communication skills, setting, media, feedback, and environment.
5. The communication and nursing processes interweave to provide the nurse with a foundation to assist clients toward optimal adaptation.
6. Empathy enables the nurse to view clients in a caring and objective manner and to interact with them in a planned, systematic way.
7. The techniques of therapeutic communication (clarification, reflection, confrontation, verification, self-disclosure, informing, silence, summarizing, directing, and questioning) are the nurse's tools to elicit helpful or facilitative interaction with the client.
8. Barriers to therapeutic communication, such as defending, lack of regard for the other person, and advising, interfere with or inhibit communication between the nurse and client.

9. Therapeutic communication is one of the most powerful tools of the psychiatric-mental health nurse.

Key Terms

Behavior
Communication
Feedback
Congruence
Clarifying
Reflecting
Confronting
Verifying

Self-disclosure
Giving information
Silence
Summarizing
Directing
Questioning
Interviewing

Teaching Strategies

1. Prior to class, develop several scenarios for students to use in dyadic work. Example: You have just begun your junior year in nursing. Last night, your good friend and roommate for the past year and a half told you that she didn't want to room with you anymore and that she didn't want to talk about it. Talk to you dyad partner about this for 5 minutes, focusing *only* on your *thoughts/content*. Using the same or a similar situation as above, direct the student to *focus only on feelings; talk about your thoughts/content, but present an incongruent feeling such as happiness.* Have all the dyads work through at least two of the same situations as speaker *and* listener, and then reconvene the group for discussion focusing on the following questions:
    a. What were your thoughts as you listened to incomplete or incongruent messages?
    b. What were your feelings as you listened to incomplete or incongruent messages?
    c. Which communication techniques would have been helpful as you recognized incomplete or incongruent messages? Give an example of how you think it may have assisted the individual; assisted you.
    d. What feedback can the message senders now give to those who "listened" to you in relation to their listening skills (*i.e.*, eye contact, physical posture, voice tone, gestures)?
    e. What was helpful to you about the listener?
    f. What was not helpful to you about the listener?
2. Prior to class, assign students to have a 10- to 15-minute conversation with a patient (or friend) discussing a problem in which they attempt to use therapeutic communication techniques. Have them write the conversation in the form of a process recording. During class, discuss the following:
    a. Which techniques seemed most easy/natural or most difficult to use? What interpersonal issues might influence this?
    b. Which techniques seemed most helpful? Why?
    c. Which barriers to communication were you aware of using? How did you know, from the patient's response, that the technique was not helpful?
    d. Is it possible that a therapeutic technique may not be helpful? If so, when and why?

e. What differences, if any, were you aware of while using therapeutic techniques, as compared with a more social, nonstructured interaction?

Supportive Materials

Anthony W, Carkhuff R: The Art of Health Care: A Handbook of Psychological First Aid Skills, pp 9–24. Amherst, Human Resource Development Press, 1978

Assey JL, Doscher S, Whiting S: The Nurse-Patient Relationship (videotape). Chapel Hill, NC, Health Sciences Consortium, 1981
(The Nurse-Patient Relationship videotape series consists of eight videotapes representing eight sessions of an 11-week (22 sessions) nurse-patient relationship. The series offers the viewer the opportunity to experience the process of a relationship between a psychiatric nursing student and a middle-aged female psychiatric patient. The average length of each videotape is 30 minutes, with a series running time of approximately 4 hours. The videotape series is accompanied by a student workbook and the instructor's guide.)

Bradley J, Edinberg M: Communication in the Nursing Context, 1st ed, pp 124–143. New York, Appleton-Century-Crofts, 1982

Hays J, Larson K: Interacting with patients. New York, Macmillan, 1963

Karshmer J: Rules of thumb: Hints for the psychiatric nursing student. J Psychosoc Nurs Ment Health Serv 20:25–28, 1982

Sayre J: Common errors in communication made by students in psychiatric nursing. Perspect Psychiatr Care 16:175–183, 1978

Chapter 5
Therapeutic Relationships

Introduction

Chapter 5 attends to the relationship between the nurse and client as being the core of nursing. The uniqueness of this therapeutic relationship is differentiated from a social relationship and an intimate relationship.

Throughout the chapter, the student is reminded of the purposefulness of the therapeutic relationship as it progresses through the introductory, working, and termination phases. Tasks of each phase are identified, as well as common reactions of the nurse and client.

Significant attention is given to behaviors and attitudes of the nurse that facilitate an atmosphere of acceptance, honesty, and trust within the relationship. The student is encouraged to recognize, appreciate, and value the need for self-awareness and the impact that the nurse's self (thoughts, feelings, and behaviors) has on the relationship and on the client's growth. Common expectations and sources of anxieties for the client and the nurse are explored.

At the conclusion of Chapter 5, the author summarizes the following major points:

1. A therapeutic relationship is one in which the nurse and client participate and work together toward the goals of meeting the client's needs and facilitating his growth.
2. There are three possible types of relationships—social, intimate, and therapeutic.
3. Therapeutic relationships progress through initial or introductory, middle or working, and termination phases.
4. The core of nursing is the relationship between the nurse and client.
5. The nurse recognizes that the client's behavior is his best possible adaptation to stress at the time.
6. The therapeutic relationship provides the client with an opportunity to examine unsuccessful adaptive (or maladaptive) behaviors and to explore and try out new adaptive skills.
7. The nurse's self-awareness, responsibility, emotional maturity, objectivity, and empathy are powerful tools of intervention.

Key Terms

Relationship	Phases of a therapeutic relationship
Social relationship	Acceptance
Intimate relationship	Transference
Therapeutic relationship	Countertransference

Teaching Strategies

1. During classroom or clinical supervision experiences, have students role-play a nurse-patient meeting in which a contract to develop a therapeutic relationship is made. Encourage observing students to give feedback based on theoretical rationale.
2. Present students with a situation such as the following:

   Mary Gordon is a 19-year-old who wants to
   quit college and marry. She is in severe
   conflict with her parents, who would like her to
   obtain a college degree and who tell
   her they will not support her in any way
   if she marries.

   Have students volunteer to role-play the context of such a situation while portraying a social interchange. Encourage students to share their thoughts and feelings after the role-playing experience and to compare and contrast therapeutic and social relationships.
3. Facilitate student responses to questions such as the following: How do you know when you can trust another person? How do you know when another person accepts you? What nursing behaviors contribute to acceptance and trust within a therapeutic relationship?
4. In the clinical setting, facilitate students in developing, maintaining, and terminating therapeutic relationships. Provide weekly supervision experiences concurrent with clinical experiences.
5. Have students record and analyze verbatim nurse-patient interactions and use therapeutic relationship theory as one source in the analysis of this record.
6. Have students discuss the needs of the chronically mentally ill in their locale. How is the community responding to these individuals? What sociopolitical forces have contributed to the positive and negative responses to the homeless?

Supportive Materials

Assey JL, Doscher S, Whiting S: The Nurse-Patient Relationship (videotape). Chapel Hill, NC, Health Sciences Consortium, 1981
(The Nurse-Patient Relationship videotape series consists of eight videotapes representing eight sessions of an 11-week (22 sessions) nurse-patient relationship. The series offers the viewer the opportunity to experience the process of a relationship between a psychiatric nursing student and a middle-aged female psychiatric patient. The average length of each videotape is 30 minutes, with a series running time of approximately 4 hours. The videotape series is accompanied by a student workbook and the instructor's guide.)

Campaniello JA: The process of termination. J Psychosoc Nurs Ment Health Serv 29–32, February 1980

Koehne-Kaplan NS, Levy KE: An approach for facilitating the passage through termination. J Psychosoc Nurs Ment Health Serv 11–14 June, 1978

Sundeen S, et al: Nurse-Client Interaction, 3rd ed, pp 155–201, 305–351. St. Louis: CV Mosby, 1985

Thomas, MD: Trust in the nurse-patient relationship. Behavior Concepts and Nursing Intervention, pp 117–125. Philadelphia, JB Lippincott, 1970

Chapter 6
Sociocultural Aspects of Care

Introduction

Chapter 6 introduces the student to a wide array of sociocultural dimensions that impact on choices made by persons during periods of health or illness. The chapter presents an in-depth exploration of the American culture, the dominant culture within our society, as well as the four large minority cultural groups within the United States (*i.e.*, Spanish-speaking, American Indian, Asian-American, and black American). Throughout the exploration of these various cultures, attention is given to attitudes, beliefs, customs, practices, and values that have implications for nursing actions.

The charge to nurses to recognize, understand, and appreciate cultural similarities and differences between the client and nurse is emphasized repeatedly in the chapter. Fulfillment of this charge impacts directly on the level of nursing care delivered and ultimately on client growth.

Chapter 6 also assists the student in applying the nursing process to clients of different cultures. The importance of the nurse's self-awareness of personal attitudes, values, and prejudices is likewise stressed.

At the conclusion of Chapter 6, the author summarizes the following major points:

1. Culture is learned behavior that is transmitted from one generation to another.
2. Culture governs an individual's patterns of action, beliefs, and feelings.
3. Awareness of cultural similarities allows health care providers to appreciate common human behaviors and bonds; failure to appreciate cultural variations results in ineffective communication and relationships between client and health care providers.
4. Health care providers are members of a subculture influenced by the values of their (in our case, American) culture, and these values are reflected in the administration of health care.
5. Enculturation is the process by which an individual learns the expected behavior of a culture; acculturation is the process whereby two cultural groups come into contact with each other.
6. Each ethnic group has a unique history.
7. The four large minority groups in the United States are Spanish-speaking Americans, American Indians, Asian-Americans, and black Americans.
8. No form of behavior can be judged normal or abnormal outside its cultural context.
9. The nurse recognizes that the quality of communication between health care provider and client directly affects the quality of health care.
10. The health care provider needs to be aware that, in some cultures, the family assumes greater importance than the individual.

11. Failure to identify the decision maker in the client's family may result in sabotage of the plan of care.
12. Nursing intervention is planned with sensitivity to the client and family's unique health needs and cultural influences.
13. Knowledge of cultural similarities and differences is essential in the delivery of quality health care.

Key Terms

Culture
Subculture
Ethnic group
Enculturation

Acculturation
Ethnic people of color
Nursing process as related to cultural factors

Teaching Strategies

1. Assist students to examine attitudes, feelings, and values that may impact on delivery of quality nursing care. Encourage completion of unfinished sentences such as the following:
   a. I dislike caring for patients who _____

   _____.
   b. People who let others dominate them are _____

   _____.
   c. Family members should visit the patient who _____

   _____.
   d. When I feel angry, I _____

   _____.
   e. My strongest prejudice is _____

   _____.
   f. If I had a serious health problem, I would _____

   _____.
   g. People who use herbs, folk medicinal practices, and so forth instead of traditional health care are _____

   _____.

   After students complete the above exercise, encourage group sharing. Facilitate discussion about how the students perceive their attitudes, feelings, and values influencing their behavior when delivering nursing care.
2. In the clinical setting, have the student identify cultural similarities and differences between themselves and their clients; identify which of the cultural similarities and differences may serve as either barriers or assists to the development of a therapeutic relationship; identify strategies for overcoming cultural differences and enhancing cultural similarities.
3. Assign students in groups of three to attend a local church service that is not affiliated with their chosen religious sect. Have them observe such aspects as the following:
   a. How do the people dress?
   b. How do the people behave?
   c. What are my thoughts in reaction to being here?

d. What are my feelings in reaction to being here?

e. What differences or similarities do I perceive from my cultural beliefs, values, or attitudes or practices?

4. Invite as guest lecturers representatives from various cultural groups within the community. Have them present information relative to their cultural norms associated with issues such as the following:

a. How are feelings such as sadness, anger, joy, and embarrassment expressed?

b. What are their beliefs about self-disclosure?

c. Whom do people within their culture "turn-to" when they are emotionally or physically ill?

d. How do they show caring within their culture?

e. What are their expectations of mental health care providers?

f. How do they define health and illness?

Supportive Materials

Brink PJ (ed): Transcultural Nursing: A Book of Readings. Englewood Cliffs, NJ, Prentice-Hall, 1976

Caudle P: Found one person. Am J Nurs 73:310–313, 1979

Mitchell AC: Barriers to therapeutic communication with black clients. Nurs Outlook 26:109–112, 1978

Part Two

The Process of Psychiatric-Mental Health Nursing

Chapter 7
Psychosociocultural
Assessment

Introduction

Chapter 7 discusses psychosociocultural assessment as the first step of the nursing process used in psychiatric-mental health nursing. Conducting a *thorough* psychosociocultural assessment integrates theoretical perspectives such as Maslow's and Seyle's views, which emphasize human needs, problems/stressors, and adaptive resources. Holism of the assessment is highlighted as the author explores a hypothesis approach to assessment that includes assessment in each of the areas of biologic, psychological, social, cultural, spiritual, and behavioral experience.

The chapter offers the student exposure to many tools that assist in the compilation of assessment data and the conduct of a thorough psychosociocultural assessment of a psychiatric client. Emphasis is given to the communicative and interpersonal skills of the nurse as being the most significant tools in the assessment process.

At the conclusion of Chapter 7, the author summarizes the following major points:

1. Nursing assessment is the gathering of client data, which are then classified and categorized in the analysis step of the nursing process.
2. Nursing assessment explores the needs, problems, and adaptive resources of the individual and the means by which the nurse may help the client move to a higher level of health.
3. Identification and clarification of the client's problems are major purposes of nursing assessment.
4. Through the hypothesis approach to assessment, the nurse interviewer explores client functioning in the psychological, social, biologic, behavioral, cognitive, cultural, and spiritual areas of their lives.
5. A variety of assessment tools should be used to conduct a comprehensive assessment of the psychiatric-mental health client.
6. The communication and relationship skills of the nurse comprise the most essential elements of the assessment interview.

Key Terms

Nursing assessment
Hypothesis approach to assessment:
    Psychological hypotheses
    Social hypotheses
    Biologic hypotheses
    Cognitive hypotheses
    Cultural hypotheses
    Spiritual hypotheses

Tools of assessment:
History
Psychological testing
Mental status examination
Client self-assessment
The interview (process and content)

Teaching Strategies

1. Divide the class into groups of three and have them, in or out of class, conduct a psychosociocultural assessment using the "Guide to Client Assessment" included in Chapter 7. One student is to function as the nurse, one as the client, and one as the evaluator. The evaluator's role is to critique and give feedback to the nurse relative to her interviewing skills. Using a Likert scale, the evaluator might be asked to evaluate the nurse's performance in such areas as the following:
   a. Listening skills
   b. Attentiveness
   c. Ability to assist the client to make transitions in his thinking
   d. Clarity of communication by interviewer (*i.e.*, was he or she clear, specific?)
   e. Ability to recognize and respond to feelings and thoughts of immediate importance to the client
   f. Ability to establish rapport with the client
2. After study of Chapter 7, facilitate students' discussion of areas of a psychosociocultural assessment that they believe will be
   a. The most difficult for them to obtain
   b. The easiest for them to obtain
   c. The most significant components of their development of a plan of care
   d. The least significant components of their development of a plan of care
   As they respond to such questions, facilitate their discussion of thoughts, feelings, past experiences,
   and so on that may impact on their responses.
3. In the clinical setting, invite a psychologist who has administered psychological tests to a patient whom the students know to discuss the purpose of the tests and the results of the patient's performance. Facilitate a discussion with the students about comparing and contrasting nursing assessment data with the results of the psychological test data.
4. After study of Chapter 7, have students seek out (*e.g.*, by means of a chart, Kardex) the psychosociocultural assessment of at least two patients whom they know. Ask them to comment on their thoughts about the psychosociocultural assessment of the two patients and critique the quality of the assessment in light of information presented in Chapter 7.

Supportive Materials

Barry P: Psychosocial Nursing: Assessment and Intervention, pp 157–168. Philadelphia, JB Lippincott, 1984

Snyder J, Wilson M: Elements of a psycholog˙ ıl assessment. Am J Nurs 235–239, February 1977

Chapter 8
Nursing Diagnosis

Introduction

This chapter discusses the second phase of the nursing process, during which the nurse analyzes client assessment data, looks for clusters of data that fit together in patterns, identifies strengths and resources of the client and family, determines the motivational readiness of the client and family for change, determines a problem list, and writes a nursing diagnosis. The nursing diagnosis is a critical component of the nursing process, because its purpose is to direct the intervention toward altering the influencing factors, or etiology, associated with the diagnosis.

The author discusses in some detail the historical development of a taxonomy for writing nursing diagnoses. The taxonomy used to make the medical diagnosis, the *Diagnostic and Statistical Manual*, 3d ed., revised (DSM III-R), is described in detail. A discussion of the interface of nursing diagnosis and DSM III-R is presented in Chapter 8, noting both advantages and pitfalls.

At the conclusion of Chapter 8, the author summarizes the following major points:

1. Analysis of the assessment data gathered for a client culminates in the determination of the most important, clearly written, definitive nursing diagnoses.
2. Clients have varying levels of motivation for change and may need help from the nurse to reduce the restraining forces and increase the motivating forces for change, increasing the client's sense of personal control.
3. Reviewing the client's strengths and resources helps determine the ability of the client to cope with his problems and assists in directing the decision regarding nursing diagnoses.
4. The nursing diagnosis is a statement of a client's response pattern to a health disruption and guides the planning and intervention phases of the nursing process.
5. The medical diagnosis is made using the criteria set in DSM III-R. The nurse can use this information in the decisions regarding nursing diagnoses.
6. DSM III-R is a theoretical multiaxial classification system that fosters a holistic approach to the client. It includes specific behavioral criteria for each diagnosis.
7. The current NANDA taxonomy of nursing diagnoses contains useful diagnoses for psychosocial nursing.

Key Terms

Analysis of data
Motivational readiness

Nursing diagnosis
NANDA taxonomy

Problem list   DSM III-R
ANA definition of nursing (1980)

Teaching Strategies

1. Have students develop a problem list for a patient they have worked with in the clinical area based on examining, synthesizing, categorizing, and evaluating data according to the patient's problems, strengths, motivations, and resources. (Refer them to Case Study: Ms. Deborah K. at the end of Chapter 8.) Have students justify to the group their problem list by discussing each step of their analysis.
2. Assign students to interact with a patient about whom they have no knowledge of the diagnosis from the chart, Kardex, or other sources and a patient whose diagnosis they know. Encourage a discussion about the advantages and disadvantages of knowing a patient's medical diagnosis, with special emphasis on the student's awareness of her own thoughts and feelings during the two interactions.
3. Have students present a seminar on the DSM III-R. Assign each student to report on at least one of the five axes in a general way and to present at least one known patient's full medical diagnosis according to DSM III-R.
4. Have students read at least one article about nursing diagnoses from the bibliography presented in Chapter 8. In addition, have them seek out (by chart, Kardex) the nursing diagnoses of at least two patients whom they know. Ask them to comment on their thoughts about the nursing diagnoses of the two patients suggested by the staff nurses, specifically recalling the errors in writing nursing diagnoses noted in Chapter 8.
5. Have students work throughout the semester refining their abilities to write nursing diagnoses on their patients, using the paradigm, *"problem statement*, related to *causative statement."*
6. Require students to do a patient presentation using the format provided in this chapter's insert, "Case Study: Ms. Ella C."

Supportive Materials

Barry P: Psychosocial Nursing: Assessment and Intervention, pp 169–172. Philadelphia, JB Lippincott, 1984

Lego S: The American Handbook of Psychiatric Nursing, pp 620–621. Philadelphia, JB Lippincott, 1984

Townsend M: Nursing Diagnoses in Psychiatric Nursing: A Pocket Guide for Care Plan Construction. Philadelphia, FA Davis, 1988.

Williams J, Wilson HS: A psychiatric nursing perspective on DSM-III. J Psychosoc Nurs Ment Health Serv 20: 14–20, 1982.

Chapter 9
Planning

Introduction

Chapter 9 explores the third step of the nursing process—planning. The author defines planning as "a structuring of (client) needs and problems in an orderly manner so that a goal may be achieved." Emphasis is given to the methodical process used when devising and executing a plan of care.

Nursing care plan components presented in Chapter 9 include diagnosis (medical or nursing), client problems, expected outcomes (short-term and long-term goals), deadlines, and nursing orders/approaches. Component parts are defined and operationalized through the use of relevant psychiatric-mental health client situations. Throughout these sections of the chapter, ongoing attention is given to the fact that the care plan is *not* developed by the nurse *for* the client; rather, it is created *with* the client in conjunction with other mental health team members and individuals significant to the client. The care plan assists the nurse to clarify her thinking, to communicate client needs/problems or change, to organize care delivery, and to measure effectiveness of performance.

In addition, the chapter addresses the value and purposes of standardized care plans in the psychiatric-mental health arena. Use of standard care plan formats assists the nurse with accountability for recognizing and responding to unique problems of the individual client. Accountability is emphasized again in the chapter's section related to the balance service system approach to client care. This approach capitalizes on health team members' being accountable to the client by facilitating continuity and consistency in care as the client enters and exits various segments of the mental health care system.

At the conclusion of Chapter 9, the author summarizes the following major points:

1. When a client seeks therapy, he is mandating change that will affect all his relationships.
2. The writing of a plan clarifies the planner's thinking and details the choices available to him.
3. Establishing time frames within the plan provides guidelines for review and evaluation of the plan.
4. Nursing care plans provide structure for care and define nursing.
5. Nursing care plans contain the nursing diagnosis, long-term and short-term goals, outcomes, deadlines, and nursing orders or approaches.
6. Standardized nursing care plans acknowledge the similarities of behavior and, therefore, allow the nurse in the workplace to focus on the client's uniqueness.
7. Consistency and effectiveness of care are promoted by a system of care planning that identifies the responsibilities of each team member.

Key Terms

Planning
Purposes of planning
Long- and short-term goals
Method as related to planning/goal achievement
Nursing care plan:
      Problem statement/nursing diagnosis
      Expected outcomes
      Deadlines
      Nursing orders/approaches
Standardized care plans
Balanced service system

Teaching Strategies

1. Using the nursing care plan format described in Chapter 9, have the students develop a plan of care for a client they have worked with in the clinical area. Have the student present the plan to the group of students by discussing each step of the plan—that is, problem statement/nursing diagnosis, expected outcomes (short-term and long-term goals), deadlines, and nursing orders.
2. After study of Chapter 9, have students seek out (*e.g.*, by chart, Kardex) the nursing care plan of at least two patients whom they know. Ask them to comment on their thoughts about the plan developed by the staff nurse. Critique the quality of the plan in light of information presented in Chapter 9.
3. Have students work throughout the semester in refining their abilities to write nursing care plans on their patients.
4. Have students comment on the pros and cons of using standardized care plans.

Chapter 10
Intervention

Introduction

Chapter 10 explores an eclectic developmental framework as the basis for the intervention phase of the nursing process. Knowledge of this framework assists the nurse in focusing intervention on a person who is dealing with specific developmentally related needs and tasks rather than on a specific diagnostic label that is "attached" to an individual.

The author presents basic tenets that serve as a foundation for an eclectic developmental approach to the practice of psychiatric-mental health nursing. Permeating the tenets are beliefs about key concepts such as human individuals, interactions, growth, maturity, and behavior.

An overview of the developmental issues, needs, and tasks of persons in the infancy through the adult stages of development are presented. Based on this theoretical knowledge of the typical or normal development, the author then relates this stage-specific theory to developmentally based nursing approaches for various psychiatric-mental health disorders (*i.e.*, schizophrenia—infancy, manic-depression—toddlerhood, neurotic disorder—preschool years, and so on).

At the conclusion of Chapter 10, the author summarizes the following major points:

1. In the treatment of psychiatric-mental health clients, it must be remembered that persons do not move from their fixation, or pathology, to maturity in one leap, but move from one level of fixation to the next higher level.
2. Underlying helping relationships is the basic belief that persons grow as a result of positive interpersonal interactions.
3. The helping person has a responsibility to be knowledgeable in varied theoretical and conceptual approaches in order to be consistent with the growth of the client.
4. The eclectic developmental approach should ultimately provide a framework to help clients resolve developmental fixations and reach the level of a mature, fully functioning person.

Key Terms

Eclectic developmental approach
Assumptions underlying an eclectic approach
Developmental issues, needs,
     and tasks (infancy-adulthood)
Developmental lags/emotional fixations
Relationship between specific diagnostic categories,
     developmental phases, and nursing interventions

Teaching Strategies

1. Have students compare and contrast the first stage of the nurse-patient relationship (Chapter 5) to the first stage of human development (Chapters 8 and 10). Have them use theory to support their discussion. Key issues focused on may include the following:
   a. Describe the theoretical rationale, using eclectic developmental theory, on which you based your choices of nursing interventions.
   b. Identify developmentally related behavioral patterns or emotional themes inferred from the patient's verbal and nonverbal data.
   c. Note a specific theory (psychodevelopmental) relative to the behavioral patterns or emotional themes inferred from the patient's verbal and nonverbal data.
   d. Evaluate the effectiveness or ineffectiveness of your intervention and give alternative interventions when necessary. (Include this objective after study of Chapter 11.)
2. Have students describe verbal and nonverbal nursing interventions that promote and maintain trust within a therapeutic relationship. Compare these interventions with interventions that would negatively impact on trust formation and maintenance. Do this same exercise for other psychosocial issues (*e.g.*, anger, dependence, control).
3. Have students use their knowledge of adaptive parenting behaviors associated with each stage of development, as well as knowledge gained from Chapter 10, to compare and contrast adaptive parenting behaviors with therapeutic nursing interventions for the developmental stages of infancy through adolescence.

Supportive Materials

Assey JL, Doscher S, Whiting S: The Nurse-Patient Relationship (videotape). Chapel Hill, NC, Health Science Consortium, 1981
(The Nurse-Patient Relationship videotape series consists of eight videotapes representing eight sessions of an 11-week [22 sessions] nurse-patient relationship. The series offers the viewer the opportunity to experience the process of a relationship between a psychiatric nursing student and a middle-aged female psychiatric patient. The average length of each videotape is 30 minutes, with a series running time of approximately 4 hours. The videotape series is accompanied by a student workbook and the instructor's guide.)

Chapter 11
Evaluation

Introduction

Chapter 11 examines the concept of evaluation from the specific perspective of its essence to the conduct of the nursing process. In addition, the examination of evaluation focuses on the broader perspective of its relevance to professional accountability and quality assurance.

Relative to the nursing process, the author purports that the target of evaluation is twofold—that is, the changes experienced by the client as a result of nursing actions and the quality or effectiveness of the nursing care itself. Evaluation of these targets in the psychiatric-mental health arena can be most elusive, difficult, and challenging, yet most significant to client growth and to effective and satisfying nursing practice.

From the broader perspective, Chapter 11 assists students with expanding knowledge of various approaches to evaluation beyond the targets pertinent to conduct of the nursing process in a psychiatric-mental health setting. Structure, process, and outcome approaches to evaluation are defined and operationalized. Of particular relevance in this section, the Standards of Psychiatric and Mental Health Nursing Practice are presented as examples of standards against which quality of care is judged.

In addition, Chapter 11 attends to the significance of quality assurance in nursing. The need to define desired client outcomes, to relate the nursing process to these outcomes, and to develop criteria to evaluate care given are identified as essential aspects of ensuring the delivery of quality care. Examples of tools and methods used by nurses to evaluate quality of care delivered include nursing histories, problem-oriented records, nursing rounds, nursing care plans, client feedback, and nursing audits.

At the conclusion of Chapter 11, the author summarizes the following major points:

1. The manifestations and long-term nature of mental illness, as well as the artful and collaborative qualities of psychiatric care, work against cause-and-effect appraisals.
2. The broader and timely issue of self-regulation aims to ensure quality in professional performance.
3. Approaches to evaluation—structure, process, and outcome—are related to quality assurance programs, the goal of which is improvement in health care.
4. Nursing histories, problem-oriented records, nursing rounds, nursing care plans, client feedback, and nursing audits are all tools or methods that can be used by nurses to maintain quality of care.

Key Terms

Evaluation

Nursing process:

    Targets of evaluation

Approaches to evaluation:

    Structure

    Process

    Outcome

Quality assurance

Professional standards review

    organizations (PSROs)

Components of a quality assurance program

Problem-oriented record

Rounds

Nursing audit

Teaching Strategies

1. Have students discuss their thoughts about such questions as the following:
   a. What is the most significant criterion that you use to evaluate the effectiveness of your nursing actions?
   b. How do you decide whether the nursing care that you deliver is effective? Efficient?
   c. Do you base effectiveness of care that you deliver on client changes? Is this always a reliable or sound measure? If so, why? If not, why not?
2. After study of Chapter 11, have students use methods presented in the chapter to evaluate care plans that they design with their patients.
3. After study of Chapter 11, have students seek out (*e.g.*, by chart, Kardex) the nursing care evaluations of at least two patients whom they know. Ask them to comment on their thoughts about the nursing care evaluations of the two patients and critique the quality of the evaluations in light of information presented in the chapter.
4. Have students attend an interdisciplinary team meeting and observe the differences and similarities between how team members evaluate client change and effectiveness of care.
5. Have students determine what quality assurance methods are used by the psychiatric-mental health unit or facility to which they are assigned. Based on their assessment and information presented in Chapter 11, have them discuss their thoughts and recommendations for change.
6. Invite, as a guest speaker, a quality assurance coordinator from a local health facility that offers mental health care to clients. Ask the coordinator to discuss the overall program used by the facility, with specific emphasis on the psychiatric area.
7. Have students interview representatives from various disciplines involved in delivering mental health care. Have them solicit opinions from these individuals about how they evaluate quality of care.

Part Three

Intervention Modes

Chapter 12
Milieu Therapy

Introduction

The psychiatric-mental health therapeutic milieu includes the people and all other social and physical factors within the environment with which the client interacts.

Concepts, characteristics, and attitudes of the milieu are described in terms of their rationale for being. For example, activities such as exercise class, jogging, and assertiveness classes are included in a therapeutic milieu in order to minimize social withdrawal and regression. The entire mental health team and its members are presented as needing attributes such as conflict resolution and a basic humanistic philosophy. Special emphasis throughout the chapter is placed on the personnel in the milieu encouraging and fostering active involvement and participation of patients in their environment.

The role of nurses in applying the nursing process is discussed in terms of their contributions to providing physical care, administering medications, providing psychosocial care, and mental health teaching. The nurse's viewing of the patient from a holistic frame of reference enables her to use her knowledge and skills to help patients meet their physiological, psychological, and social needs. The author views the nurse as the primary manager and coordinator of milieu activities.

At the conclusion of Chapter 12, the author summarizes the following major points:

1. From a stress-adaptation framework, clients may require milieu therapy in a hospital setting as a result of a decreased ability to cope with, and adapt to, life stressors.
2. The therapeutic milieu provides a temporary, safe haven from these life stressors while also offering clients opportunities to acquire adaptive coping behaviors; that is, the therapeutic milieu affords asylum, in the truest sense of the word, while simultaneously extending an invitation to clients to return to the mainstream of living and being in the world.
3. Essential characteristics of a therapeutic milieu include individualized treatment programs, links with the client's family and community, effective relationships among members of the mental health team, and humanistic attributes of the mental health team members.
4. Milieu therapy is a group therapy approach that uses the client's total living experience as the primary therapeutic agent.
5. Nurses have traditionally assumed responsibility for managing and coordinating therapeutic milieu activities, and they also serve as a link between clients and the socially constructed reality of everyday life.
6. One important nursing function in the therapeutic milieu is mental health teaching of clients (*e.g.*, information about psychotropic medications, psychiatric disorders,

interpersonal and communication skills, stress management, relaxation therapy, and so forth).

7. Nurses in the therapeutic milieu must communicate the following message by their every action and word: Come, come join us in the world. You are welcome here.

Key Terms

Milieu
Mental health team
Milieu therapy
Attitude therapy

Teaching Strategies

1. After visiting a psychiatric-mental health setting, have the students list every component of the milieu observed using the following categories: people, social activities/facilities, and physical activities/facilities.

2. Discuss the author's statement, ". . . the therapeutic milieu affords clients refuge while also supplying them opportunities to acquire adaptive coping skills." Ask the students to personalize this quote to patients they are familiar with. Specifically, from what or whom might their patient need a safe haven? What opportunities does their patient's milieu offer (or not offer) to acquire needed adaptive coping skills?

3. Have students identify all members of the mental health team in their clinical placements. Are there deficiencies?

4. Have students identify the six elements that characterize a therapeutic milieu. Discuss activities of each element in which the nurse might be involved. Ask for specific examples. Example: Progressive levels of self-responsibility—might this element influence how and when medications are given to patients?

5. Have students observe or participate in a recreational activity with a patient or patient group. Ask them to write a one-page paper on the experience, focusing on their thoughts and feelings about how the activity is considered "therapeutic."

6. Ask students to make an appointment with and spend 15 to 30 minutes with at least one (nonnurse) member of the mental health team, discussing that person's role, responsibilities, functions, and philosophy of psychiatric-mental health care. Have the student group share their experiences.

7. Have students write a mini-care plan identifying a patient problem, goal, and intervention for each of the following categories of nurse responsibilities: providing physical care, providing psychosocial care, administering medications; and mental health teaching. Refer to the chapter for sample care plans.

8. Have students identify the classification levels/levels of responsibility utilized on their clinical units. Discuss patients known to students in regard to the patients' identified classifications on the unit.

9. Discuss patients whom students are familiar with and identify the patients' predominant behavioral styles. Have the students then suggest which attitude (from attitude therapy) would be most helpful to assume in interactions with the patient.

10. Discuss the pros and cons of attitude therapy.

Chapter 13
Individual Psychotherapy

Introduction

Psychotherapy is an open-ended process involving two people (client and therapist) that aims to assist clients to change the ways they think, feel, or behave in relation to themselves and others. A choice to make change, to understand oneself more, or to get relief from pain commonly precipitates a person's entering an alliance with a therapist.

Within Chapter 13, the author differentiates psychotherapeutic relationships from other human relationships. The student is guided to think about the boundaries of such relationships, as well as the ethical responsibilities of therapists. Issues such as the therapist's objectivity, perspective, and specialized knowledge base are explored. Also, therapeutic qualities of congruence, unconditional positive regard, and accurate empathic understanding are examined as essentials to facilitating the client's growth and change. In addition, a comparison of client and therapist expectations of therapy is offered.

Chapter 13 also explores the origins of therapy, various levels of therapy (*i.e.*, supportive, reeducative, reconstructive), and classic stages of psychotherapy. Relevant concepts to the psychotherapeutic process (*i.e.*, insight, resistance, transference, counter-transference, ambivalence) are defined and operationalized.

At the conclusion of Chapter 13, the author summarizes the following major points:

1. A person may choose to engage in the process of psychotherapy to treat an emotional disorder, to deal with problems, or to gain insight and self-understanding.
2. Various levels of psychotherapy (supportive, reeducative, and reconstructive) describe the depth of therapy and the degree of change undertaken by the client.
3. During each of the three stages of individual psychotherapy, the client and therapist have certain tasks to accomplish, such as exploring the client's history and current problems and needs during the introductory stage.
4. Because of their objectivity, perspective, and specialized knowledge, therapists can generally be more effective than a person's family or friends in helping clients deal with problems and growth needs.
5. Client and therapist need to communicate clearly their expectations of each other and therapy.
6. The important concepts of psychotherapy, such as insight, repression, resistance, and reworking, are explored and applied to the client involved in individual psychotherapy.

Key Terms

Psychotherapy
Levels of therapy:
    Supportive
    Reeducative
    Reconstructive
Stages of psychotherapy:
    Introductory
    Working
    Working through
Therapist qualities:
    Congruence
    Unconditional positive regard
    Accurate empathic understanding
Insight

Repression
Free association
Resistance
Reworking
Transference
Countertransference
Ambivalence
Ambiguity
Object constancy
Acting in
Acting out
Interpretation
Working through
Translating

Teaching Strategies

1. Have students read a book that focuses on a psychotherapeutic relationship. Examples of books include the following:
   Axline V: *Dibs in Search of Self*
   Gordon M: *I'm Dancing As Fast As I Can*
   Green H: *I Never Promised You a Rose Garden*
   Linder R: *The Fifty Minute Hour*
   Rossner J: *August*
   Rubin T: *Jordi, Lisa and David*
   Have students present either a verbal or written book report that includes addressing objectives such as the following:
   a. Describe the client's reason for entering therapy and expectations of therapy.
   b. Describe positive and negative qualities of the therapist and how these were exemplified in the therapeutic process.
   c. Discuss how the therapist fulfilled or did not fulfill the ethical role responsibilities.
   d. Discuss your perception of how at least five concepts of psychotherapy, which were presented in Chapter 13, were exemplified in the psychotherapeutic relationship.
2. Have students interview health care team members who represent various disciplines (*i.e.*, nursing, medicine, psychology, social work) and gain their perspective of issues such as the following:
   a. What do you perceive as the purposes of psychotherapy?
   b. How do you define your role as a therapist?
   c. What do you believe are the impacts of the relationship that you have with clients?
   Have students compare and contrast responses gained from the persons representing various disciplines.
3. Encourage student discussion in response to questions such as the following:
   a. How do you define psychotherapy?
   b. Why do you believe *most* people enter therapy?

c. What do you believe are the rights and responsibilities of the client in therapy? Of the therapist?

d. Do you believe that it is ever acceptable for the therapist to become the client's friend? Give your rationale.

e. Do you believe that the therapist ever has the right or responsibility to terminate a therapeutic alliance with a client? Give your rationale.

4. Over the time period of the course in which this content is offered, view with students, preferably in small seminar groups, the nurse-patient relationship videotapes suggested in the Supportive Materials section below. View one videotape a week and, on conclusion of the viewing, facilitate discussion of topics/questions such as the following:

a. Identify the stage of the nurse-patient relationship. Give verbatim data to support your thinking.

b. How did the nurse demonstrate qualities such as congruence, unconditional positive regard, empathy, and acceptance? Give verbatim data to support your thinking.

c. Give examples of how the psychotherapeutic concepts defined in Chapter 13 were evidenced.

d. If you were the nurse in this relationship, identify at least two segments of the videotape and explain how you would have felt and what you would have been thinking during the meeting.

5. Encourage students to discuss their thoughts in response to the "Research Update: The Effectiveness of Psychotherapy" insert in Chapter 13. Also, have them select one article from the nursing literature that reports findings of research that focus on client outcomes in response to psychotherapy. Have them present a verbal synopsis of the article to their peers.

Supportive Materials

Assey JL, Doscher S, Whiting S: The Nurse Patient Relationship (videotape). Chapel Hill, NC, Health Sciences Consortium, 1981
(The Nurse-Patient Relationship videotape series consists of eight videotapes representing eight sessions of an 11-week (22 sessions) nurse-patient relationship. The series offers the viewer the opportunity to experience the process of a relationship between a psychiatric nursing student and a middle-aged female psychiatric patient. The average length of each videotape is 30 minutes, with a series running time of approximately 4 hours. The videotape series is accompanied by a student workbook and the instructor's guide.)

Assey JL, Whetsell I: Memorandum. J Psychosoc Ment Health Serv 35–36, July 1980

Doona ME (ed): Travelbee's Intervention in Psychiatric Nursing, 2d ed, pp 137–162. Philadelphia, FA Davis, 1979

Sayre J: Common errors in communication made by students in psychiatric nursing. Perspect Psychiatr Care 16:175–183, 1978

Chapter 14
Groups and Group Therapy

Introduction

An understanding of group dynamics and their application is essential for the psychiatric-mental health nurse in order to function effectively while working with health team members and with patients and their families. This chapter discusses groups in terms of characteristics, types, norms, leadership styles, decision-making processes, roles, and stages. It examines the advantages and disadvantages of group therapy in general and the theoretical frameworks for group therapy, such as Rogerian, Gestalt, and transactional analysis in particular. The author also includes guidelines to determine the therapeutic benefit of a growth or therapy group for an individual participant. Although the author presents therapeutic group interventions, she notes that the use of therapeutic communication techniques with groups requires that nurses possess considerable preparation and skill in group work.

At the conclusion of Chapter 14, the author summarizes the following major points:

1. A group is three or more persons with related goals.
2. Groups vary according to their size, homogeneity of membership, climate, norms, and goal directedness.
3. Group norms are the patterns of interaction that develop over time within a group.
4. A group leader designs the group's structure, style of leadership, and decision-making policies.
5. Roles in groups are task, building and maintenance, and individual roles.
6. The advantages of group therapy include its effectiveness and efficiency in time and cost.
7. Nurses participate as leaders and co-leaders in multiple formal and informal groups.
8. Most therapeutic group experiences can be categorized as psychotherapy or growth groups.
9. The three stages of group development are the initial, working, and termination stages.
10. Nurses and other group leaders employ a variety of therapeutic interventions with groups, and they identify and explore latent versus manifest and process versus content communication.

Key Terms

Group
Primary groups
Informal groups

Secondary groups
Formal groups
Altruism

Community support groups

Power

Authority

Autocratic

Democratic

Laissez-faire

Decision making

Universality

Catharsis

Latent content

Manifest content

Content

Process

Transference

Countertransference

Teaching Strategies

1. Have students prepare a genogram of themselves in their family of origin and a short description of their major personality attributes in relation to their sibling position (see the second and third listings in Supportive Materials). Have students then discuss how the characteristics of their primary group (their family) influenced how they were socialized into future groups and how they adopt various roles in groups.

2. Have students evaluate the norms of their supervision group in terms of role expectations, sanctions, taboos, and references to power and authority.

3. Have students discuss the advantages and disadvantages of using the three leadership styles during the following psychiatric-mental health situations.
    a. Patient group planning recreational activities for the coming week
    b. Community meeting discussing complaints about the dietary department
    c. Patient group on an outing at a shopping mall
    d. Patient group in the living area at the time a suspicious and resistant patient is being admitted and shown around the unit.
    e. Assisting a patient group to prepare to go to group therapy or occupational therapy
    f. Patient group brought together because of a patient's accusation that money was stolen from her

4. Identify a "leader" of the group for this exercise. Then give the leader the following scenario written on a piece of paper.

    John is married to Ruth. John is a traveling salesman and is often out of town overnight. John went on a trip and was to return the next day. While John was gone, Ruth went across the river to spend the night with her lover, Ted. In the morning, Ruth tried to return home before John got back from his trip. When she went to cross the bridge over the river, there was a "wild man" on the bridge who said that he would kill anyone who tried to come over the bridge. Ruth went back to her lover, Ted, for help, but he refused. She then went to her best friend Carla's house, telling her what had happened and asking for help, but she refused. Ruth then tried to cross the bridge alone, and the "wild man" killed her.

    Who is the *most* responsible for Ruth's death, excluding the "wild man"? John? Ruth? Ted? or Carla? And who, of these same people, is the *least* responsible?

    Before leaving the room, tell the leader and the group that they have 20 minutes to discuss the scenario and come up with a decision about the two questions. Tell them that the two decisions *must* be made by *consensus*.

    After the decisions are made, discuss with the group the following:
    a. What are the advantages and disadvantages of a consensus decision?

b. How did the leader and each group member see themselves meeting their responsibilities during the decision-making process? (Refer to those delineated in Chapter 14.)
5. Have the students evaluate you, anonymously if preferred, as their instructor in terms of the group leader's responsibilities in structuring their supervision group during the first day. (Refer to the discussion about "structuring the group" in Chapter 14.)
6. During the final supervision group, have the group evaluate themselves and every other group member according to the member roles they played *most often* during the time they were together. Use the following format, and have members give feedback to each other. Include yourself.

Instructions:　Consult the chapter for task, maintenance, and individual group roles. For each member, place checkmarks in the columns corresponding to the roles he or she played *most often* in the group. Include yourself.

	Members' Names											
I. Group task roles a. Initiator-contributor												
b.												
c.												
etc.												
II. Group maintenance roles a. Encourager												
b.												
c.												
etc.												
III. Individual roles a. Aggressor												
b.												
c.												
etc.												

Supportive Materials

Charrier GO: Cog's ladder: A model of group development. In Pfeiffer JW, Jones JE (eds): The 1974 Annual Handbook for Group Facilitators. La Jolla, University Associates, 1974

Miller S, Winstead-Fry P: Family Systems Theory in Nursing Practice, pp 43–52. Reston, Va, Reston Publishing, 1982

Toman W: Family Constellation, 3d ed, pp 153–194. New York, Springer, 1976

Wilson S: Introduction to Group Process: Member Behaviors in a Group (21-minute audiovisual cassette). Chapel Hill, NC, Health Sciences Consortium, 1983.

Chapter 15
Families and Family Therapy

Introduction

Systems theorists are now focusing less on disturbed families and more on successful families in an effort to understand how stress and change affect the lives of all families as they strive to adapt. The author defines "family" in its broadest terms, including many nontraditional configurations. The discussion includes family functions, developmental stages, and structure. Family communication theory (Satir, Beavers) and family systems theory (Jackson, Bowen, Minuchin, and others) are described. A significant portion of Chapter 15 describes and discusses the many developmental, physical, social, cultural, and political stressors that impact on families. Finally, the steps of the nursing process are applied to functional and dysfunctional families, with the author's admonition that family therapy is undertaken by nurse-therapists who have undergone formal training in family therapy during graduate or postgraduate education.

At the conclusion of Chapter 15 the author summarizes the following major points:

1. A family is a culturally produced social system made up of two or more people in a primary group.
2. Stages of family development may depend on the adult members or the oldest child as an index of family development.
3. According to the family systems theory, the whole (the family) is more than the sum of its parts (the members of the family).
4. Living systems possess clear but open boundaries, negentropy, differentiation, and adaptation.
5. Successful families produce competent people through mature leadership by parents.
6. Historical, developmental, role-related, and environmental stressors influence today's family.
7. Assessment of families includes examination of the family's open system orientation, boundaries, contextual clarity, power, encouragement of autonomy, affective tone, negotiation and task performance, transcendent values, and health.
8. Goals planned for optimal to troubled families are enhancement of existing strengths, anticipatory guidance, parenting education, and holistic health measures.
9. Nurses working with families need to possess self-understanding, empathy, therapeutic communication skills, and knowledge of family theory.
10. The family therapist assists the family to identify and express their thoughts and feelings, define family roles and rules, try more productive styles of relating, and restore strength to the parental coalition.

Key Terms

Family

Emerging family

Crystallizing family

Integrating family

Actualizing family

Family structure

Family function

Boundaries

Negentropy

Entropy

Adaptation

Optimal families

Adequate families

Midrange families

Troubled families

Double bind

Scapegoating

Family therapy

Differentiation

Teaching Strategies

1. Have students prepare their own genogram (refer to the first entry under Supportive Materials) and identify (a) their stage of family development and (b) the critical issues facing their parents and the oldest sibling.

2. Have students describe a family they know that is different from their family in terms of structure, function, communication patterns, rules, and linking. Have them elaborate on the differences as they may relate to the adaptive capabilities of that family.

3. Have students make case presentations to the group, describing the family characteristics of the patients with whom they are familiar. The format for the presentations should follow Beavers's eight variables critical for producing competent people.

4. Have students identify the stressors that impacted on their families in the 40s, 50s, 60s, 70s, and 80s and discuss those in relation to the adaptive/functional strengths or weaknesses of their families.

5. Have students discuss how they did or did not see their parents meet their own physical, social, and emotional needs as adults or spouses. In what way were they as children influenced?

6. Ask students to watch television for 1 week, keeping a brief diary describing ways in which the family is presented. Discuss observations as a group.

7. Invite guest speakers from the community to discuss the stresses and problems of raising families. Examples: white, middle-class parents; black or white divorced mother; black or white divorced father; aunt/grandmother parent or parents; parents with adopted children; single, unmarried parent.

8. Invite a group of children or adolescents, including those living with both parents and those living with one divorced parent, and have them discuss some of the advantages and disadvantages of their family situation. Have the students develop a list of questions they would like to have the children respond to.

9. Using the family assessment guides in Chapter 15, have the students present a family whom they observed or interacted with. If possible, have students observe a family therapy session to do this exercise.

Supportive Materials

Miller S, Winstead-Fry P: Family Systems Theory in Nursing Practice, pp 43–52. Reston, Va, Reston Publishing, 1982

Toman W: Family Constellation, 3d ed, pp 153–194. New York, Springer-Verlag, 1976

Chapter 16
Behavioral Approaches

Introduction

Chapter 16 focuses on the beliefs, purposes, principles, goals, and various approaches associated with the modality of behavior therapy. Those espousing behaviorism place little, if any, emphasis on the cause of maladaptation, but rather focus on assisting persons to enhance adaptation by learning ways to alter their responses to the environment.

While introducing the student to principles of behavior therapy, such as classical conditioning and operant conditioning, the author highlights the various individual contributions to the field (*e.g.*, Pavlov, Watson, Eysnick, and Wolpe) as well as illustrates the application of these principles to clinical situations. In addition, specific terms including *extinction*, *prompting and fading*, and *shaping* are defined and operationalized.

A section of the chapter is devoted to addressing and illustrating the similarities between the nursing process and the application of behavioral principles in treatment. Also, the student is introduced to behavioral approaches, including contracting, imagery, behavioral rehearsal, and assertiveness training.

At the conclusion of Chapter 16, the author summarizes the following major points:

1. Following a complete data collection, which includes health history, physical and mental status examinations, lab tests, and client and family interviews, objective observation of the maladaptive behavior for a period of time is essential for accurate behavioral assessment.
2. The health team documents the observation period and the frequency of the behavior.
3. Specificity, a key factor in behavioral analysis, results from objective systematic approaches to client problems.
4. Descriptions of both adaptive and maladaptive behaviors and behavioral outcomes must be detailed in performance expectation to allow precise measurement and evaluation.
5. Behavioral interventions, including behavioral contracting, cognitive therapy, modeling, imagery, assertiveness training, and progressive muscle relaxation, are powerful approaches to client problems and needs.

Key Terms

Behaviorism

Behavior therapy

Classical conditioning

Reciprocal inhibition

Operant conditioning

Generalization

Discrimination

Extinction

Prompting and fading
Shaping
Reinforcers
Contracting
Cognitive therapy:
    Rational emotive therapy
    Thought stopping

Modeling
Imagery
Behavior rehearsal
Assertiveness training
Problem solving
Muscle relaxation

Teaching Strategies

1. Invite a behavior therapist from the community to deliver a presentation, from a case study point of view, which primarily focuses on problem identification, interventions (including rationale for interventions), and evaluation.

2. Have students compare and contrast the philosophies of the treatment approaches presented in Chapters 13 and 16. Have students address questions such as the following:
   a. What are the similarities and differences of the two approaches?
   b. Are there clients with certain types of maladaptations who might gain more from one approach than the other? Give rationale and examples of clients to support your response.
   c. What philosophical stance "fits" more with you as a person? Support your position with your thinking.

3. Using the assertive techniques presented in this chapter, have students (in dyads) role-play the following situations:
   a. Your roommate asks you to lend her or him a dollar. You have a dollar, but do not want to lend it. Refuse your roommate.
   b. Your head nurse asks you to work overtime this coming Friday evening. You have a date and do not want to work. Refuse your head nurse.
   c. You are working with a subordinate on a nursing unit. It is your job to make the assignment for the subordinate. You do, but she whines and does not want to do what you tell her.
   d. Confront your friend who is working on a class project with you about the fact that her part of the project is late.
   e. You and your friend think and feel very differently about the issue of abortion. Discuss the issue for 5 minutes.

Chapter 17
Psychopharmacology

Introduction

Chapter 17 focuses on the topic of psychopharmacology and its relevance to psychiatric-mental health nursing. The major groups of psychoactive drugs (*i.e.*, antipsychotic, antidepressant, anxiolytic, and antimanic), including their desired effects, adverse and side-effects, normal dosage range, and nursing implications, are discussed in detail. Also, drug interactions and contraindications are presented.

The psychiatric-mental health nurse's role and responsibility in interfacing with clients who are being treated with medication is stressed. The nurse's responsibility to the client includes functioning from a sound, up-to-date knowledge base of psychopharmacology. This knowledge base is paramount to the nurse's ability to engage in safe administration of medications (*e.g.*, recognize desired and adverse drug effects, normal dosages, contraindications). Nurses also have the responsibility to teach the client and family members about the client's medication.

At the conclusion of Chapter 17, the author summarizes the following major points:

1. The introduction of psychotropic agents has revolutionized the treatment of institutionalized psychiatric clients and has facilitated their return to community life.
2. One of the more important theories of the action of psychotropics is based on the biochemical activities of the neurotransmitters, specifically norepinephrine and dopamine.
3. The psychotropic medications are classified into the antipsychotic or neuroleptic, antidepressant, anxiolytic, and antimanic agents.
4. Nurses play a significant role in the development of new information from research studies of psychotropic drugs.
5. Noncompliance with medication regimens is a major problem in the field of psychiatric-mental health care.
6. One of the variables that may reduce this noncompliance with regimens and may prevent recurrences of emotional disorder is client and family teaching, an integral part of the psychiatric treatment plan.
7. The revolution that heralded the advent of psychopharmacology several decades ago has developed into continuous research processes that lead to the important drug discoveries of today and tomorrow.

Key Terms

Compliance vs. noncompliance
Antipsychotic agents/neuroleptics
    Movement disorders
        Pseudoparkinsonism
        Akathisia
        Dystonia/dyskinesia
        Tardive dyskinesia
Antiparkinsonism medication
Neuroleptic malignant syndrome
Antidepressant agents
    Tricyclic antidepressants
    Monoamine oxidase inhibitors
Anxiolytic agents
Antimanic agents

Teaching Strategies

1. Have students be responsible for knowing the actions, therapeutic dosages, uses, side-effects, toxic effects, routes of administration, contraindications, and nursing implications for *all* drugs being administered to their clients. Also, have students address the question of how the medication impacts either positively or negatively on the nurse-client relationship.
2. In order to help students gain a fuller perspective of some of the unpleasant side-effects experienced by individuals who have to take psychoactive drugs, have each student talk with at least five psychiatric-mental health clients who are receiving psychoactive drugs. Encourage them to ascertain from the clients their:
   a. History with taking psychoactive drugs.
   b. Experiences with side-effects and adverse effects. For example, "When you say that your mouth felt dry, tell me what that was really like for you," or "When you say that you had trouble passing your urine, what exactly does that mean?"
   c. Experiences related to what helped them "get beyond" the unpleasant side effects.
   d. Knowledge regarding why they are taking psychoactive drugs.
3. Regardless of the clinical settings used, require students to come to the clinical area with drug cards for each category of psychoactive drug. Information on the card includes the areas proposed in teaching strategy 1 above. Have students be responsible for knowing this information.
4. Assign students to observe and participate in "client drug education" sessions, which may be ongoing in clinical settings used for their experiences. Have them critique these sessions for their usefulness to clients, as well as their accuracy of content.
5. Have students discuss their thoughts and feelings about psychopharmacologic research using psychiatric-mental health clients as subjects. What is the nurse's role in informed consent?
6. Have students assess their client's (and family's) knowledge regarding the medications they are taking.

Supportive Materials

DeGennaro M, Hymen R, Crannell AM, Mansky PA: Antidepressant drug therapy. Am J Nurs 1304–1310, 1981

Harris E: Lithium. Am J Nurs 1311–1315, 1981

Harris E: Antipsychotic medications. Am J Nurs 1316–1323, 1981

Irons P: Psychotropic Drugs and Nursing Intervention, pp 11–26. New York, McGraw-Hill, 1978

Gotz D, Gotz V: Drugs and the elderly. Am J Nurs 1347–1351, 1978

Skidmore-Roth L: Medication Cards for Clinical Use. New York, Appleton-Century-Crofts, 1986

Part Four

Developmental Issues in Psychiatric-Mental Health Nursing

Chapter 18
Development of the Person

Introduction

Chapter 18 discusses, in depth, the development of the person while focusing on five different developmental theories: intrapsychic, interpersonal, social learning, cognitive, and behaviorist. Special emphasis is placed on developmental phases or stages along various continuums. Student nurses are encouraged to understand the factors influencing human development and to formulate a conceptual framework of mental health problems and treatment approaches.

At the conclusion of Chapter 18, the author summarizes the following major points:

1. Human development is a complex and multifaceted process involving a variety of forces that effect unique personalities.
2. Development is currently considered to be a continuous process of unfolding throughout the life span, rather than being limited to a few years in early life.
3. No longer is the responsibility for development placed on the mothering person alone, but on the complex and interacting influences on the individual.
4. The developmental period of old age is a focus of current attention. Evidence supports the idea that a qualitative level of development continues in the increasing numbers of elderly persons in our population.
5. Healthy, adaptive adult function occurs at a level of interdependency.

Key Terms

Oral phase
Anal phase
Phallic phase
Latent phase
Genital phase
Integrating tendencies
Trust–mistrust
Autonomy–shame and doubt
Initiative–guilt
Industry–inferiority
Identity–role confusion

Intimacy–isolation
Generativity–stagnation
Integrity–despair
Sensorimotor
Preoperational
Concrete operational
Formal operational
Contemplative recognition
Representational intelligence
Consonance
Dissonance

Teaching Strategies

1. Have each student write at least one memory they have or story they have been told about themselves that they can relate to each of Freud's phases of psychosexual development. Ask students to share one memory with the group while giving their theoretical rationale for identifying it with the phase chosen.

2. Have students develop a list of words, phrases, or sentences that they believe describe their personality at this time. Information gained from parents, peers, and others may be included in the list. Discuss the following questions with them in class:

   a. With what developmental phase, according to Erikson, do the ego qualities noted on their list correspond? Is there overlap at all (*i.e.*, might they be in transition)? Have students justify their responses with a theoretical rationale.

   b. What developmental tasks do they need to work on before moving to the next phase?

   c. What problems/issues are they vulnerable to, given incomplete or inadequate/negative resolution of their present phase?

   d. What are the major differences between Freud's, Sullivan's, and Erikson's theories of personality development?

   e. How might an understanding of the various developmental theories assist the nurse in understanding, planning, and evaluating care?

3. Direct students to spend at least 30 minutes with a preschool child, talking to them and observing their behavior. In class, ask students to discuss their experiences with the child from a cognitive theoretical (Piaget) point of view.

4. Prior to class, develop a list of psychosocial problems that may be encountered in a psychiatric-mental health setting. Include both inpatient and community situations, and emphasize those of the adult and aged. Present the list to the class and ask students to suggest goals, interventions, and methods of evaluations. All interventions suggested *must* be justified with theoretical rationale. An example format for discussion follows:

Patient Data	Identified Problem	Goals	Nursing Interventions	Methods of Evaluation

Supplemental Materials

Lidz T: The Person. New York, Basic Books, 1968

Sundeen S, et al: Nurse-client interaction, 3rd ed, pp 34–59. St. Louis, CV Mosby, 1985

Chapter 19
Sexuality and Sexual Concerns

Introduction

Sexuality is an integral part of the personality, and therefore, issues related to patients' sexual concerns and problems need to be fully understood by the professional nurse in order to assist in the facilitation of adaption. Chapter 19 presents an in-depth discussion of sexuality and sexual concerns throughout the life span. A humanistic perspective emphasizes the importance of identifying the patient's sexual norms and needs. Content is specific and detailed and notes various physical and emotional dysfunctions. The role of the nurse in assisting various patients is discussed, with specific focus on the use of the nursing process.

At the conclusion of Chapter 19, the author summarizes the following major points:

1. The sexual nature of the personality affects the emotional, spiritual, and psychological natures of the self; indeed, they are not separate "natures," but parts of the personality, the self.
2. Sexual development is influenced by genetic and hormonal factors and by the development of gender identity.
3. The human sexual response cycle consists of four phases—desire, excitement, orgasm, and resolution.
4. Traditional and alternative sexual life-styles, such as homosexuality, transsexuality, and paraphilias, are contrasted.
5. Clients who undergo injury or surgery resulting in a changed body image often suffer a blow to their sexual identity.
6. Nursing interventions with clients whose physical or mental disorders interfere with their sexual abilities include client and family teaching, support, and counseling.
7. Sex therapy may be the treatment of choice for certain common sexual problems— erectile dysfunction, rapid ejaculation, vaginismus, and orgasmic dysfunction.
8. The steps of the nursing process are applied to clients with sexual problems.

Key Terms

Sexuality
Sensuality
Sex roles
Gender role
Sexual identity
Sex derivative
Sex adjunctive
Sex arbitrary

Paraphilias
Cunnilingus
Fellatio
Coitus
Transsexual
Dyspareunia
Erectile dysfunction
Vaginismus

Teaching Strategies

1. Have students write one statement about themselves in response to each of the following words:
   a. Sexuality
   b. Sensuality
   c. Sex role
   d. Gender identity
   Ask students to verbally share any or all of their responses and discuss how they differentiated one term from another.

2. Ask students to discuss their thoughts and feelings about people who engage in sexual activity for the purpose of
   a. Procreation—to conceive children
   b. Relationship strengthening
   c. Recreation—play and personal enjoyment
   Have students then discuss
   a. How much, if any, religious values influenced their responses? In what way?
   b. What other variables may have influenced their responses? In what way?
   c. How might their own thoughts and feelings help or hinder their ability to assist patients with differing points of view?

3. Have students discuss the early experiences in their lives that influenced the development of their gender. Have them recall experiences of other (e.g., siblings, friends) that seemed to influence other's gender roles to develop differently from their own.
   Examples:
   a. Relationship and availability of same-sex parent
   b. Relationship and availability of opposite-sex parent
   c. Relationship and availability of significant others, such as aunts, uncles, grandparents, older siblings, teachers, heroes

4. Have students anonymously fill out the following sentence-completion exercise. Compile the *group's* results and encourage a discussion of the answer in an effort to both desensitize the subject matter and also present a broader picture of the person's sexual beliefs.
   Exercise:
   a. Sex is only permissible _____.
   b. Masturbation is _____.
   c. Cunnilingus is _____.
   d. Fellatio is _____.
   e. Anal intercourse is _____.
   f. Homosexuality and lesbianism are _____.

5. Have students discuss the following situation:
   Ms. Rowan is a 43-year-old mother of five children. She has been admitted to the inpatient psychiatric unit for chronic depression. Her husband was recently admitted to the coronary care unit (CCU) with a myocardial infarction. Ms. Rowan has been involved in a lesbian relationship with Karen T. for the past 18 months. Karen visits Ms. Rowan daily, and they spend their time in Ms. Rowan's room during the visits. Ms. Rowan's children also visit, and during these times, they all go visit Mr. Rowan in the CCU.

You are the charge nurse on this unit. What are your thoughts and feelings? Do you see these thoughts and feelings as being helpful or not to Ms. Rowan? What areas or issues in relation to unit life might you anticipate? How can you be most helpful to Ms. Rowan? How can you be most helpful to possibly angry or threatened staff members?

6. Discuss and practice nursing interventions for situations in which the behavior of the patient appears to be seductive. (Refer to the first entry under Supportive Materials.)

7. If the program is available in your area, assign students to view *Good Sex* with Dr. Ruth Westheimer on Lifetime Cable Network, on their own, or have videotapes made and watch together for the purpose of identifying common sexual concerns of the public.

8. Have students list all the myths about sexuality addressed in Chapter 19. Discuss. Example: There is no more prevalence of sexual dysfunction, bizarre sexual practices, child molestation, or sadomasochistic sexual activity among homosexuals, lesbians, and bisexuals than that found among heterosexual groups.

9. Discuss student's thinking on and /or observations of the issues of sexuality and sexual needs of psychiatric clients (both in and out of the hospital).

Supportive Materials

Assey J, Herbert J: Who is the seductive patient? Am J Nurs 531–532, April 1983
Schwartz S, Shockley E: The Nurse and the Mental Patient, pp 157–166. New York, Russell Sage Foundation

Chapter 20
Mental Health of the Aging

Introduction

Since the beginning of this century, the number of elderly persons in the United States has been continuously increasing. A significant nursing response to the growth in this sector of the population was the American Nurses' Association's recognition of geriatric nursing as a significant specialty area (1966) and development of Standards for Geriatric Nursing Practice (1970). These events affirm the fact that nurses have a responsibility to know, understand, and respond to the physical and psychosocial needs of elderly persons.

Early in Chapter 20, the author raises issues that assist the nurse in examining their beliefs about the elderly and their attitudes toward them. Recognition of these personal issues can assist the nurse with improving the delivery of care offered to the elderly client.

The aging process and accompanying physiological changes are examined, with respect to each body system (*e.g.*, respiratory, cardiovascular, gastrointestinal). Significant body changes, as well as implications for nursing care, are identified throughout the discussion. Also, pertinent psychosocial considerations of aging are examined. Efforts are made to help the reader dispel myths about unproductivity, disengagement, and inflexibility associated with aging.

Relative to nursing care, the author emphasizes the nurse's role in health promotion and assisting the elderly person to adapt to changes associated with growing old. Special attention is given to preventive and therapeutic measures such as life review therapy and life-cycle therapy groups, which aid with the adaptation process and have the potential of enhancing the elderly person's quality of life.

In addition, the author briefly explores the nodal events of retirement and residential placement as two possible occurrences that confront some elderly persons. Depression among the elderly, including behaviors that may indicate suicidal ideation, are discussed.

At the conclusion of Chapter 20, the author summarizes the following major points:

1. Aging is a process of continual physiological change from birth to death and a continual developmental growth process.
2. Through an understanding of the normal aging process, the nurse is better able to assist the elderly to comprehend the inherent physiological and psychological changes and to cope with these changes through adaptation.
3. The nurse is urged to recognize the myths or stereotyped attitudes about aging and to become aware of her own attitudes toward, or beliefs about, the aged.
4. Nursing provides the elderly with the opportunity to continue to grow throughout the process of aging and to meet death as a person at peace with himself.
5. Loneliness, the threat of retirement and residential placement, and depression and the possibility of suicide are powerful stressors to the elderly.

6. Treatment of the cognitively and emotionally impaired elderly include reality orientation, remotivation, resocialization, reinforcement, and milieu, attitude, self-image, and reality therapies.

Key Terms

Elderly
Aging process
Myths of aging

Life review therapy
Life-cycle group therapy

Teaching Strategies

1. After study of Chapter 20, facilitate student discussion of the questions for discussion that follow the Case Study: Mrs. W. and Therapeutic Dialogue—Life Review Therapy.

2. Using the Psychosocial Assessment Guide presented in Chapter 20, have students interview an elderly person of their choosing. After completion of the assessment, have them identify nursing diagnoses and propose interventions.

3. Have students project that they're an elderly person and write a paper or a poem to nurses who are not elderly and perhaps do not appreciate what it's really like to be elderly. Have students share with "these nurses" exactly what it's like to be elderly, who I (the elderly person) really am, and so on. (Refer to the poem at the beginning of the chapter.)

4. Divide the students into dyads. Have students reminisce with one another about the different thoughts, feelings, meanings, and memories that are triggered by events such as the following:
   a. High-school graduation
   b. First date
   c. Death of a significant other
   d. Pictures from their wallets

   Have students share with one another the importance that the event had for them and what they might have learned from it. What, if any, impact did the event have on their life? After completion of the exercise, have the students discuss the potential value of using such an exercise with an elderly client.

5. Have students complete unfinished sentences such as the following:
   a. To grow old is _____.
   b. The most positive aspect of aging is _____.
   c. The most negative aspect of aging is _____.
   d. Living in a nursing home is _____.
   e. Society's treatment of the elderly is _____ because _____.

6. Have students interview at least three elderly persons to ascertain what being elderly is like for them. Have students incorporate into their interview the stereotyped attitudes about the elderly that are included in Chapter 20. For example, they might pose questions such as the following:
   a. Tell me about the people you currently enjoy being with the most.
   b. Tell me about the last time you felt really sad (or really angry, or really happy, and so on).

c. For you, what's the best (the worst) thing about being elderly?
d. Talk about some memories that are important to you.
After the interviews, have the students report on positive and negative views of aging that were evident during each interview. How did the individual elderly person's view seem to impact on his or her life?

Supportive Materials

Hamner ML: Insight, reminiscence, denial, projection: Coping mechanisms of the aged. J Gerontol Nurs 10:66–68, 81, 1984
Hernan J: Exploring aging myths. J Gerontol Nurs 10:31–33, 1984
Brower HT: Do nurses stereotype the aged. J Gerontol Nurs 11:17–28, 1985
Burnside I: Psychosocial issues in nursing care of the aged. J Gerontol Nurs 7:689–694, 1981
Burnside I: Working with the elderly group process and techniques. Monterey, Wadsworth Health Sciences Division, 1984 (At the conclusion of each chapter, the author has suggested exercises, as well as resources [films, audiovisuals, tapes/cassettes, organizations].)

Chapter 21
Anxiety and Anxiety Disorders

Introduction

Anxiety, an inevitable part of the lives of all humans, is a response to psychic threat. As such, anxiety is a subjective experience of the individual and cannot be observed directly. However, the effects of anxiety can be observed behaviorally and physiologically. Chapter 21 addresses anxiety as a human phenomenon that may occur in mild, moderate, severe, or panic levels. If an individual experiences intense anxiety over substantial periods of time, the psychiatric condition known as anxiety disorder is said to be present. Anxiety disorders may present in one of the following five types: phobic disorders, panic disorder, generalized anxiety disorder, obsessive-compulsive disorder, or posttraumatic stress disorder. The author of Chapter 21 discusses the five anxiety disorders in terms of their major signs and symptoms. Additionally, nursing care pertinent to anxiety-disordered individuals is presented within the framework of the nursing process.

At the conclusion of Chapter 21, the author summarizes the following major points:

1. Anxiety is a clinical feature of almost every psychiatric syndrome.
2. Anxiety occurs as the initial response to psychic stressors and is ascertained through self-reports, such as feelings of dread, apprehension, restlessness, and "jitteriness," and through physiological signs, such as increased heart rate and blood pressure, excessive perspiration, sexual dysfunction, and increased rate and depth of respiration.
3. Levels of anxiety range from mild to moderate, severe, and panic.
4. An anxiety disorder is a psychiatric condition characterized by the emotion of intense terror and thoughts of impending catastrophe that persist over substantial periods of time.
5. Phobic disorders commonly seen in clinical practice include agoraphobia, social phobia, and simple phobia.
6. A panic disorder is an anxiety disorder characterized by recurrent anxiety attacks of panic proportions that occur unpredictably.
7. Generalized anxiety disorder is usually characterized by a level of chronic anxiety that is so uncomfortable that it interferes with a person's daily living.
8. In obsessive-compulsive disorder, the individual experiences recurrent obsessions, or persistent thoughts, ideas, images, or impulses, and compulsions, or ritualistic behaviors, that he or she feels compelled to perform in a routinized manner.
9. Posttraumatic stress disorder is the development of certain characteristic symptoms after exposure to a traumatic life experience capable of psychologically harming most persons.
10. Planning and implementing nursing care for clients with anxiety disorders center on

helping the individual to accept the experience of anxiety as normal and inevitable, increase self-awareness regarding variations in anxiety levels, reduce shame about exhibiting signs of anxiety, learn and apply self-help techniques to reduce anxiety, and increase problem-solving and coping skills.

Key Terms

Anxiety:
    Mild
    Moderate
    Severe
    Panic
Behavioral patterns:
    Withdrawal
    Acting out
    Psychosomatization
    Avoidance
    Problem solving

Types of anxiety disorders
Phobic disorders:
    Agoraphobia
    Social phobia
    Simple phobia
Panic disorder
General anxiety disorder
Obsessive-compulsive disorders:
    Obsession
    Compulsion
Posttraumatic stress disorder

Teaching Strategies

1. In relation to themselves, have each student describe the following:
   a. Typical behavioral, physiological, and cognitive effects of anxiety
   b. Examples of stressors that have precipitated anxiety
   c. Usual ways of coping with anxiety
2. A programmed instruction entitled "Anxiety Recognition and Intervention" appears in the *American Journal of Nursing*, Vol. 65, No. 9, September 1965. Have students self-pace themselves through this classic and excellent learning program. After students complete the program, discuss key aspects of the program in class or seminars.
3. Peplau identifies the four levels of anxiety as mild, moderate, severe, and panic. Based on assessments of patients in the clinical area, have students give examples of the behavioral, perceptual, and cognitive effects of each level. Discuss appropriate nursing interventions for each level of anxiety.
4. Have students select one anxiety disorder and review the literature on it. Based on the literature review, have them orally, or in writing, present the following:
   a. Characteristics of the disorder
   b. Etiology or developmental dynamics of the disorder
   c. Course of the illness
   d. Modalities effective for treatment of the disorder

Supportive Materials

Burd S: Effects of nursing intervention in anxiety of patients. In Burd S, Marshall MA (eds): Some Clinical Approaches to Psychiatric Nursing. New York, Macmillan, 1963

Smith MC: The client who is anxious. In Lego S (ed): The American Handbook of Psychiatric Nursing, pp 387–390. Philadelphia, JB Lippincott, 1984

Tuma A, Maser J: Anxiety and the anxiety disorders. Hillsdale, NJ, Lawrence Erlbaum Associates, 1985

Part Five

Application of the Nursing Process to Disturbed Behaviors

Chapter 22
Maladaptation:
The Personality Disorders

Introduction

Narcissism seems rampant in today's society. This focus on love of self greatly overshadows many individuals' love for humanity. Accompanying this focus on self, there seems to be a noticeable increase in the incidence and prevalence of the personality disorders. The chapter begins with a general description of the personality disorders in terms of common characteristics, cause, and their relation to the health-illness continuum. The author then attempts to give the student a framework to apply the assessment step of the nursing process to specific personality disorders by discussing, in detail, the relationship between anxiety and perception, cognition, affect, behavior, and level of adaptation. Specific personality disorders such as compulsive, passive-aggressive, antisocial, paranoid, schizoid, and border-line are then described from this framework. Finally, planning and implementing nursing care for individuals with personality disorders are discussed by way of key concepts such as trust, limit setting, confrontation, and self-awareness. Nursing diagnoses are also suggested.

At the conclusion of Chapter 22, the author summarized the following major points:

1. Maladaptive personality patterns or styles may be described as a personality disorder.
2. The behavior of individuals with personality disorders is often narcissistic, dependent, depressed, egocentric, immature, hostile, and manipulative.
3. Compulsive personality disorder is marked by narrow perceptual focus, intellectual rigidity, anxiety and ambivalence, lack of mirth, inflexible stubborness, and attempts to control others.
4. The person with a passive-aggressive personality perceives others and the world in general pessimistically, is indecisive and ambivalent, feels unappreciated and misused, and procrastinates or works inefficiently.
5. Antisocial personality disorder is characterized by hostility, antagonism, punitiveness, mistrust, callousness, and insensitivity.
6. Paranoid personalities display pervasive suspiciousness, cognitive disturbances ranging from ideas of reference to delusional systems, hypercritical attacks on others, hostility, projection, guardedness, jealousy, and emotional coldness.
7. Schizoid personality disorder is marked by social withdrawal and extremely shy behavior, impoverished thought processes, indifference, and underresponsiveness.
8. The individual with borderline personality disorder uses many maladaptive patterns to avoid anxiety—splitting, avoidance, withdrawal, acting out, and psychosomatization.

9. Nursing care of clients with personality disorders requires that nurses develop a high degree of self-awareness, form trusting relationships with clients, and use counterprojection, time-out, confrontation, and limit-setting techniques, as well as other therapeutic approaches.

Key Terms

Personality
Personality disorders:
    Compulsive personality
    Passive-aggressive personality
    Antisocial personality
    Paranoid personality
    Schizoid personality
    Borderline personality
Behavioral patterns:
    Splitting
    Projection
    Passive-aggression

Acting out
Narcissism
Dependency
No-win relationship style
Interventions:
    Counterprojection
    Taking time out
    Confrontation
    Limit setting

Teaching Strategies

1. Invite to class or visit a psychologist or psychiatrist working in a penal system and discuss the incidence and prevalence of personality disorders in inmates. Discuss common behaviors of the inmates, as well as approaches and interventions used by staff/guards.
2. Have students review the diagnoses of patients admitted to an inpatient psychiatric unit for the past 3 to 6 months, and also for a 3- to 6-month period 10 years ago. Have students discuss their observations in terms of personality disorders.
3. Have students observe one or two soap operas for a period of 1 week. Ask them to identify and describe any personality disorders they observed, keeping particularly in mind the common characteristics of personality disorders. Discuss as a group.
4. Ask students to identify characteristics in themselves or in persons with whom they have had contact that are *similar* to those described for the personality disorders of compulsive, passive-aggressive, antisocial, paranoid, schizoid, and borderline persons. Students' discussion should include proper terminology, as well as use of the framework of perception, cognition, affect, behavior, and level of adaptation. Also, discuss the *differences* identified and discuss what impact these differences may have on their overall life functioning and satisfaction.

Supportive Materials

Carser D: The defense mechanism of splitting: Developmental origins, effects of staff, recommendations for nursing care. J Psychosoc Nurs Ment Health Serv 21–28, 1979

Lyon G: Limit setting as a therapeutic tool. J Psychosoc Nurs Ment Health Serv 17–24, 1970

Maynard C, Chitty K: Dealing with anger: Guidelines for nursing intervention. J Psychosoc Nurs Ment Health Serv 36–41, 1979

Chapter 23
Disorders of Mood:
Depressed and Manic Behavior

Introduction

Feelings associated with depression and mania are not foreign to any human being, whether healthy or ill. The difference in the feelings experienced is one of degree and intensity rather than in kind. Chapter 23 addresses the feelings, cognitive experiences, and disturbed behaviors that characterize persons who are depressed or who are manic.

The beginning sections of the chapter focus on the incidence and possible causes of depression and mania, including biologic and psychosocial influences. The health-illness continuum approach is used to assist the student with thinking about various types of affective disorders. For example, at the health end of the continuum one might conceptualize grief and mourning reactions, whereas at the illness end of the continuum, major psychotic depressions are found.

Chapter 23 emphasizes the application of the nursing process to persons suffering from disturbances in mood. The nurse's role and responsibility in primary, secondary, and tertiary prevention of disorders of mood are explored.

At the conclusion of Chapter 23, the author summaries the following major points:

1. Mood disorders, described early in recorded history, are a major mental health problem in the United States.
2. The cause of causes of mood disorders have not been established with any certainty; theories include both biologic and psychosocial influences.
3. Mood disorders can be chronic as well as acutely psychotic and can be masked by various maladaptive behaviors, such as alcoholism and promiscuity.
4. Manic behavior is psychodynamically perceived as a defense against depression.
5. The nurse has a responsibility to participate in the primary prevention of mood disorders as well as in the secondary and tertiary prevention.
6. The nurse is a collaborator with other members of the health care team, including the client and his family, and assumes an influential role in determining the client's care and treatment, which have both psychosocial and biological components.
7. Nursing assessment and intervention for the depressed client focus on the client's physical health and safety, feelings about himself and others and the expression of these feelings, and distorted perceptions and false beliefs about the environment and himself.
8. Suicide, frequently an outcome of depression, can be prevented.
9. Nursing assessment and intervention for the manic client focus on the client's

physical health, channeling of the client's energy, environmental manipulation, and reinforcement of reality.

10. Somatic therapy, including chemotherapy and electroconvulsive therapy, is a vital component of the treatment plan for a client with a disturbance in mood.

11. Nurses and other mental health professionals need opportunities to express, explore, and resolve their feelings of anger and frustration that may develop as a result of their work with depressed and manic clients.

Key Terms

Depression
Mania
Hypomania
Cyclothymic disorder
Dysthymic disorder
Psychosis
Bipolar disorder
Unipolar depression
Postpartum depression

Involutional melancholia
Agitated depression
Retarded depression
Endogenous depression
Exogenous (reactive) depression
Flight of ideas
Illusion
Hallucination
Insight

Teaching Strategies

1. Have students define, compare, and contrast the terms *mood* and *affect*. (Use resources other than the text to do this.)

2. Have students discuss the rationale and implications for nursing care behind statements such as the following:
   a. When working with a *severely* depressed client, the nurse must often take a very directive approach.
   b. It is not useful for the nurse to maintain a cheerful, happy-go-lucky attitude or try to talk a severely depressed client out of feeling sad.
   c. The risk of suicide increases as the depressed client's mood improves.
   d. The nurse has the responsibility to respond to the positive part of the ambivalence experienced by a suicidal client.
   e. Mania is a defense against depression.
   f. The manic client is extremely sensitive to environmental stimuli, and the nurse must keep such stimuli to a minimum.
   g. The manic client's physiological well-being is at risk.
   h. Responding to the manic client's latent (implied) communication is essential.
   i. Consistency in approach among team members is critical in caring for a manic client.
   j. The manic client's judgment ability frequently is impaired.

3. Have students ascertain what the suicidal precaution policies are on the units where they obtain clinical experiences. Have them critique these, proposing changes if necessary. Have them give the rationale for proposed changes.

4. Have students obtain the consent form for electroconvulsive therapy used on units where they obtain clinical experiences. Does the form explain the nature and purpose of the procedure, the risks involved, and the possibilities of complications that may occur? Have them critique the form, proposing changes if necessary. Have them give the rationale for the proposed changes.

5. Have students ascertain which antidepressant drugs are used most frequently on the clinical unit to which they are assigned. Have them query staff and patients relative to the most frequent side-effects and beneficial effects reported and experienced. Have them determine the monthly costs of specific antidepressant drugs or lithium for patients. In seminar, facilitate the discussion of their findings.

6. Have students answer and discuss the following statements in dyads for 30 minutes and then rediscuss as a group for 30 minutes:
   a. The most frightening thing to me about working with a depressed client (and about working with a manic client) is _____
   _____.
   b. My idea of what a severely depressed (and an acutely manic) person feels like inside is _____
   _____.
   c. I believe I can be helpful to a depressed client (and to a manic client) because __
   _____.
   d. When working with a depressed client (and with a manic client), I will have the most trouble with _____
   _____.
   e. People who attempt or succeed with suicide are _____
   _____.
   f. My beliefs about electroconvulsive therapy are _____
   _____.

7. In the clinical setting, have students interact with a client diagnosed as depressed and with a client diagnosed as manic. In seminar, facilitate their discussion of the following:
   a. Thoughts and feelings experienced during the interaction
   b. Impact of their own thoughts and feelings on the interaction
   c. Thoughts, feelings, and behavior of the clients that suggested depression or mania
   d. Nursing diagnoses and client behavior outcomes that were developed
   e. Therapeutic interventions that were employed

8. View videotapes 3 and 4 of the Nurse-Patient Relationship videotapes series (see Supportive Materials, below). After viewing, facilitate student discussion of the following questions:
   For videotape 3 (patient displays hypomanic behavior):
   a. Analyze the effects of the promotion of trust and cite the rationale behind the nurse's directness when she told the patient that "she would not be able to go on the outing. . . ." (In the analysis, use nurse-patient relationship theory as well as knowledge gained from Chapter 23.)
   b. Identify the major themes communicated by the patient and develop a nursing care plan (themes including loss, dependency, regression).
   For videotape 4 (patient displays depressive thoughts, feelings, and behavior):
   a. Identify two major themes communicated by the patient and give verbatim verbal or nonverbal behavioral examples of the themes. (Themes include loss, helplessness and hopelessness, regression.)
   b. Identify clues to suicidal thoughts that the patient exhibited or discussed prior to the nurse intervening with a no-suicide contract.
   c. Identify the patient's psychodevelopmental stage and discuss how the numerous

losses the patient feels in her life at this time relate to the psychodevelopmental task of the identified stage.

Supportive Materials

Assey JL, Doschet S, Whiting S: The Nurse-Patient Relationship (videotape). Chapel Hill, NC, Health Sciences Consortium, 1981
(The Nurse-Patient Relationship videotape series consists of eight videotapes representing eight sessions of an 11-week (22 sessions) nurse-patient relationship. The series offers the viewer the opportunity to experience the process of a relationship between a psychiatric nursing student and a middle-aged female psychiatric patient. The average length of each videotape is 30 minutes, with a series running time of approximately 4 hours. The videotape series is accompanied by a student workbook and the instructor's guide.)
Field WE: Physical causes of depression. J Psychosoc Nurs Ment Health Serv 7–11, October 1985
Hamrick SA, Sarasin R: The 24-hour stay. J Psychosoc Nurs Ment Health Serv 23–25, April 1986
Mulaik J: Nurses' questions about electroconvulsive therapy. J Psychosoc Nurs Ment Health Serv 15–19, February 1979
Thomas SP: Uses and abuses of electric convulsive shock therapy. J Psychosoc Nurs Ment Health Serv 17–23, November 1978
The Depressed Client. New York, American Journal of Nursing
(This film uses the health-illness continuum approach for conceptualizing depression. Vignettes of depressed client situations are related. Nursing interventions are emphasized.)

Chapter 24
Retreat from Reality:
The Schizophrenic Disorders

Introduction

It is thought that 25 percent of all hospital beds in the United States are occupied by patients whose diagnosis is schizophrenia. Attacking its population in the prime of their lives and creating major obstacles to life satisfaction, schizophrenia is a major health problem of such proportions that it is rated third in terms of morbidity, preceded only by cancer and cardiovascular disease. Additionally, the physical, psychological, and financial impact of the disease on family members makes schizophrenia one of the most dreaded and researched psychiatric disorders of our day. It is therefore imperative for any nurse working in the psychiatric-mental health field to be knowledgeable and skillful in working with schizophrenic individuals and their families. Chapter 24 addresses the essential information needed by the nurse for such work. The schizophrenic disorders are discussed in terms of incidence, cause, and diagnostic categories. Application of the nursing process to the patient with a schizophrenic disorder is focused on in great detail. Assessment and nursing diagnosis address the areas of thinking, feeling, and social/behavioral disturbances. Planning and goal setting emphasize flexibility and creativity. Interventions proposed again focus on the disturbances in thinking, feeling, and behavior. In this section, important therapies such as individual, group, behavior, milieu, and pharmacologic are presented. Finally, a useful section discussing the nurse's feelings and attitudes while working with schizophrenic patients is included.

At the conclusion of Chapter 24, the author summarizes the following major points:

1. Because it is estimated to affect 1 percent of the population and its onset occurs during adolescence and young adulthood, schizophrenia is considered a common and tragic emotional disturbance or group of disturbances.
2. The biologic theories are built on data that support genetic, biochemical, immunologic, or structural influences on the client and his behavior.
3. The psychosocial theories of the etiology of schizophrenia focus on the intrapersonal and interpersonal factors that lead to its development.
4. The five types of schizophrenia — disorganized, catatonic, paranoid, undifferentiated, and residual—have been explained in terms of their operational criteria.
5. Assessment and nursing diagnosis of the client are approached by examining the three major areas of disturbances of thinking, disturbances of feeling, and disturbances of behavior.
6. The foundation of an accurate assessment is a nonjudgmental attitude and careful, objective observation and description of client behaviors.

7. The psychiatric-mental health nurse is involved in treatment planning as a collaborative effort with other members of the mental health team, which includes the client and his family or significant others.

8. Specific goals and outcomes are set for, and with, the client and his family to intervene in the present behavior and to begin preparation for discharge to the community.

9. The nurse is encouraged to be consistent and genuine in her approach to the schizophrenic client.

10. Current treatment approaches promote the positive aspects of the family on the schizophrenic member through providing information about the disorder, available treatments, and their respective benefits and risks.

11. The nurse's own feelings while working with the schizophrenic client must be addressed openly because they are an important part of the therapeutic process.

12. Individual, group, and family therapy, the behavioristic approach, milieu therapy, and chemotherapy are discussed as useful modalities.

13. Interventions are proposed and advocated with high-risk populations, such as the children of psychotic parents.

14. Evaluation of nursing intervention is the continuous process of examination and assessment of the therapeutic effectiveness of each specific intervention.

Key Terms

Double-bind communication
Chronic schizophrenia
Subchronic schizophrenia
Process schizophrenia
Magical thinking
Neologisms
Illusions
Hallucination
Affect

Positive symptoms
Negative symptoms
Reactive schizophrenia
Associative disorder
Depersonalization
Cryptic language
Delusion
NAMI

Teaching Strategies

1. Have students make a collage from magazine pictures exhibiting representations of Bleuler's four A's: associative disturbances, affective disorder, autism, ambivalence. Discuss during and after the preparation of the collage.

2. Have the student group break into two sections and make a formal debate presentation of the following issue: Cause of schizophrenia: biologic or psychosocial? Ask each student to research at least two articles for their side of the debate issue and make bibliography cards. After the presentation, make photocopies of all cards and give them to each member of the group.

3. Have five students research the diagnostic classifications (DSM III-R) of the disorganized, catatonic, paranoid, undifferentiated, and residual schizophrenic classifications as well as the *common* characteristics of all schizophrenics. Ask them to come to the next supervision group as a person representing that classification (include attention to dress, speech, behavior, thought patterns, and so on). Spend the first 20 minutes of the group with those five members and the rest of the supervision group as if you were all attending a group therapy session. After 20

minutes, discuss questions such as the following:
   a. What is the interpersonal cost of being schizophrenic?
   b. What behaviors of the five were most difficult to deal with and be with for themselves *and* the other, noncasted members of the group?
   c. How might schizophrenia influence a person's life? Work? School? Marriage? Family?
4. Have students assess their community's resources for assisting the schizophrenic individual *and* family for (1) hospitalization, (2) outpatient therapies, (3) transition housing, and (4) independent living. Discuss what impact the strengths and weaknesses of the community has on discharge and discharge planning of schizophrenics and their families.
5. Have students contrast schizophrenia with autism, childhood schizophrenia, paranoid state, and multiple personality.
6. Have students read one of the following books throughout the semester and use a group supervision to present reports:
   Greene H: *I Never Promised You a Rose Garden*
   Beers C: *A Mind That Found Itself: An Autobiography*
   Torrey EF: *Surviving Schizophrenia: A Family Manual* (see References)
7. If possible, have students interact with a chronic and an acute schizophrenic. Compare and contrast disturbances in thinking, feeling, and behavior. Have students develop a care plan for the different needs of (1) an acutely ill, hospitalized schizophrenic and (2) one who is currently in remission and may be living in transitional housing.
8. Have students answer and discuss the following statements in dyads for 30 minutes and then rediscuss as a group for 30 minutes:
   a. The most frightening thing to me about schizophrenia is _____ _____.
   b. The most frightening thing about working with a schizophrenic patient is _____ _____.
   c. I believe I can be helpful to a schizophrenic patient because _____ _____.
   d. When working with a schizophrenic patient, I will have the most trouble with __ _____.
   e. The mother of a schizophrenic is_____ _____.
   f. I believe I can be most helpful to family members of schizophrenics by _____ _____.
   g. The therapeutic interventions I believe I will use the most while working with schizophrenics are _____ _____.
   h. My idea of what a schizophrenic feels like inside is _____ _____.
9. Have students read and respond to "A Family's View of Chronic Mental Illness" in Chapter 24.
10. Identify your local chapter of the National Alliance for the Mentally Ill (NAMI) and have students attend a meeting and report back to the group.
11. Have students identify which of the five access community support models for the care of the chronically mentally ill is operational in your locale. Investigate this

resource and, if possible, observe a caseworker during several hours of their day.

Supportive Materials

Barile L: The client who is hallucinating. In Lego S (ed): The American Handbook of Psychiatric Nursing, pp 446–448. Philadelphia, JB Lippincott, 1984

Barile L: The client who is delusional. In Lego S (ed): The American Handbook of Psychiatric Nursing, pp 450–454. Philadelphia, JB Lippincott, 1984

Harris E: Antipsychotic medications. Am J Nurs 1316–1323, 1981

Messecar R (producer): Schizophrenia: Removing the Veil (slides and audio cassette No. 366-2). Pleasantville, NY, Ibis Media, 1983

Wright L: A symbolic tree: Loneliness is the root; delusions are the leaves. J Psychosoc Nurs Ment Health Serv 30–35, May/June 1975

Chapter 25
Suspicious, Hostile, and Aggressive Behavior: The Delusional and Acting-Out Disorders

Introduction

Suspicious, hostile, and aggressive behaviors are often those manifested by patients in response to illness, injury, or hospitalization. These behaviors are demonstrated in all clinical categories and are certainly not the exclusive rights of those persons diagnosed with a mental disorder. Therefore, Chapter 25 is useful to all nurses who practice, although the chapter's focus on the mentally ill patient acts as a special reminder to the psychiatric-mental health nurse that an understanding of, and a competence in dealing with, suspicious, hostile, and aggressive behavior must become a tool in her clinical practice armamenteria.

This chapter defines and discusses delusional (paranoid) and acting-out disorders by first defining suspicious, hostile, aggressive, and acting-out behaviors. A discussion of incidence, causative theories, and dynamics of each behavior is then presented. Finally, the nursing process is applied to the behaviors. Additional highlights of the chapter include sections on diagnosing the suspicious client, inpatient treatment for an impulsive and aggressive young adult (case study), use of restraints and seclusion, and the feelings and attitudes engendered in the nurse while working with delusional (paranoid) and aggressive patients.

At the conclusion of Chapter 25, the author summarizes the following major points:

1. Etiologic theories from diverse frameworks are advanced to explain the origins of suspicious, hostile, and aggressive behavior and to guide intervention strategies.
2. The dynamics of hostility and suspiciousness, impulsivity and acting out, and anger and aggression explain the "how" and "why" of these behaviors.
3. The nurse assessing the client with paranoid or acting-out disorders gathers information about altered cognitive or perceptual states, increased psychomotor activity, altered mood or affect, environmental factors causing increased anxiety levels, and history of poor impulse control or drug abuse.
4. The nurse determines the client's ability to remain in control of his behavior.
5. In planning treatment, the nurse and client choose desired client behavior outcomes based on the needs for trusting relationships, social responsibility, and increased self-esteem.

6. Defusing and deescalating rising feeling states and supporting the client who attempts to control his behavior in socially sanctioned ways are preferable to reactionary handling of aggressive incidents.
7. When control is an issue, manipulation is a possibility.
8. A blending of the nurse's theoretical orientation with client needs leads to interpersonal, behavioral, or cognitive interventions.
9. As a member of the multidisciplinary mental health team, the nurse communicates her observations and interventions to other team members toward the goal of maintaining a consistent, holistic approach to the client.
10. Working with suspicious, hostile, and aggressive clients taps surface and deep emotions in the nurse and other mental health care providers.
11. Evaluation entails a close examination of both client and nurse to determine whether client behavior outcomes were met and to decide what nursing skills and attitudes might be more effective in helping delusional and acting-out clients reach their desired outcomes.

Key Terms

Suspicious behavior

Anger

Acting-out behavior

Chemical restraints

Hostility

Aggression

Manipulation

Teaching Strategies

1. Prior to any clinical supervision group, have the students perform the programmed instruction guide noted in the second entry under Supportive Materials.
2. In order to have students better understand some of the cultural influences in relation to the expressions of anger, have them give at least two examples of situations in which they felt angry, and ask them to describe their behaviors. Have them then deduce what they learned as a child in terms of the "proper" way to deal with angry feelings. Also, have them discuss thoughts and feelings regarding the proper way to deal with anger with a least one person whom they have observed who deals with anger differently from themselves. Have students also note the defense mechanisms they observe in themselves and others as they attempt to deal with the anxiety related to feelings of anger.
3. Discuss the relationship between anger/hostility and suspiciousness. Might these two emotions be two sides of the same coin? Elaborate using theoretical rationales *and* clinical examples.
4. Have students compare and contrast the dynamics of hostility and suspiciousness, impulsivity and acting-out, and anger and aggression. What issues do they have in common? What are the essential differences?
5. Have students assume that they are charge nurses on the 3 to 11 shift of a 20-bed, adult, inpatient, open psychiatric unit. Ask them to respond to the following questions:
   a. What behaviors or cues from a patient or patients might be indicators of a need to intervene? Include behaviors in the categories of thinking and perception, motor activity, mood, or affect, physical state, and context.

b. What knowledge or skills do you possess to assess or recognize suicidal or homicidal potential?

c. What knowledge or skills do you have to prevent violence on the unit?

d. What interventions are you aware of that could help patients prevent impending loss of control? What resources might you have to assist you on the unit?

e. Assume that a patient has lost control and is involved in an assaultive incident. List your immediate steps to apply external controls. What factors would you consider as you evaluate your nursing interventions?

6. Ask students to find out what the protocols are on their units in relation to (1) plan of action for applying external controls and (2) use of restraints and seclusion. Discuss as a group.

Supportive Materials

Assertiveness in nursing: Part I. Am J Nurs 417, 434, 1983

Understanding hostility. Am J Nurs 2131–2150, 1976

Barile L: The client who is suicidal. In Lego S (ed): The American Handbook of Psychiatric Nursing, pp 398–403. Philadelphia, JB Lippincott, 1984

Herbener G: How to control your anger: Your own and others. Nurs Life 42–45, Nov/Dec 1982

Lamb J, Rodgers D: Assisting the hostile, hospitalized child. Matern Child Nursing 336–339, 1983

Moritz D: Understanding anger. Am J Nurs 81–83, 1978

Stewart A: Handling the aggressive patient. Perspect Psychiatr Care 16:228–232, 1978

Webster M: Assessing suicide potential. In Lego S (ed): The American Handbook of Psychiatric Nursing, pp 28–33. Philadelphia, JB Lippincott, 1984

Zillman MA: Use of seclusion and restraints. In Lego S (ed): The American Handbook of Psychiatric Nursing, pp 522–527. Philadelphia, JB Lippincott, 1984

Zillman MA: Suicide precautions. In Lego S (ed): The American Handbook of Psychiatric Nursing, pp 528–529. Philadelphia, JB Lippincott, 1984

Chapter 26
Substance Abuse:
The Drug Dependencies

Introduction

Chapter 26 presents an in-depth examination of the deleterious physical, psychological, social, and behavioral effects experienced by persons who abuse or become dependent on drugs (including alcohol). Relating the choice to abuse or depend on substances to Selye's stress/adaptation syndrome framework is one of numerous causative considerations presented. The relationship between multiple factors, such as personality traits, genetic influences, culture, and environment, and persons who abuse substances is explored.

The chapter also focuses on specific drugs (*e.g.*, alcohol, barbituates, opiates, amphetamines and cocaine, hallucinogens, cannabis), criteria used to diagnose abuse or dependency problems, and particular physical, behavioral, and family consequences related to the abused substance. Throughout the discussion in this section of the chapter, numerous significant definitions of terms related to drug abuse and dependence are offered.

Application of the nursing process to the client who abuses or depends on substances is explored. The author emphasizes the need for nurses to be aware of personal attitudes and feelings while working with clients experiencing substance-abuse problems and to recognize the need to approach these persons with respect, compassion, and gentle firmness. Numerous intervention methods are identified, including Antabuse treatment, methadone maintenance, aversion conditioning, and Alcoholics Anonymous.

At the conclusion of Chapter 26, the author summarizes the following major points:

1. Selye's theoretical framework of the stress/adaptation syndrome may be applied to the problem of substance abuse and dependency.
2. There is no single etiology of drug abuse and dependence; rather, theories examine multiple factors such as personality traits, genetic influences, social, cultural, ethnic, and environmental factors, and a self-destructive phenomenon.
3. Drug dependence may be viewed as a way of coping with life's stressors by individuals who abuse substances.
4. Substance-use disorders are divided into the diagnoses of substance abuse and substance dependency.
5. Substance-induced organic mental disorders generally include intoxication, withdrawal, and delirium.
6. Each class of substances of abuse is described in terms of its effects, patterns of abuse, diagnostic criteria, organic mental disorders, and medical consequences.
7. A nonjudgmental, objective approach is essential for establishing rapport with individuals who abuse substances.

8. Rehabilitation and eventual recovery are the focus of treatment planning and intervention with individuals who abuse or are dependent on drugs.
9. Problems of substance abuse and dependency are encountered in all areas of nursing practice.

Key Terms

Psychoactive substance-abuse disorder
Psychoactive substance-induced
    organic and mental disorders
Physical dependence (addiction)
Psychological dependence (habituation)
Tolerance
Cross-tolerance
Synergism
Antagonistic effect
Additive effect

Potentiation
Blackout
Intoxication
Withdrawal
Withdrawal delirium
Amnestic disorder
Hallucinosis
Dementia
Flashbacks

Teaching Strategies

1. Have students identify resources in their community that are available to persons/families coping with substance-abuse problems. Have students obtain information from at least one resource relative to its purpose, its methodology with providing help, the population it serves, and the way in which a nurse would make a referral. Compile this information and make it available for students' present and future work with substance-abusing persons/families.
2. Have students identify national resources available to persons/families coping with substance-abuse problems. For example, have a student call 1-800-COCAINE and learn what services this resource provides. Have students share their findings with the group.
3. Have students read at least one current article related to each of the major drug categories presented in Chapter 26. Require an annotated bibliography on these readings.
4. Have students attend a meeting of Alcoholics Anonymous or an affiliated group during the course in which this content is presented. Require a written report of this experience. The write-up is to focus on the student's thoughts and feelings regarding the experience.
5. Preferably in a small group (10 or fewer students), have students complete the unfinished sentences below and facilitate group discussion on completion of the exercise:
   a. An alcoholic/substance abuser is _____
   _____.
   b. The most frightening thing to me about being an alcoholic/substance abuser would be_____
   _____.
   c. I believe that alcoholics/substance abusers can _____
   _____.
   d. The most difficult part of caring for an alcoholic/substance abuser would be ____

e. I believe that the use of methadone in treatment is (or is not) _____ _____.

f. The worst drug to be addicted to is _____
because _____.

g. My feelings toward a person being habituated versus addicted to drugs is _____
_____.

h. Society's approach toward drug abusers is _____
and should be _____.

i. If I read on a patient's chart that he or she drank approximately 1/2 pint of
alcohol per day, I would feel _____
and think _____.

6. Have students investigate the existence of "impaired nurse" programs in their community/state. Invite a speaker from this organization to the group.

7. Have students investigate their state board of nursing policies, procedures, and programs for the identification of (and intervention with) alcoholic and/or substance-abusing nurses.

8. Have students read and write (anonymously) a reaction to "Autobiography of a Recovering Alcoholic Nurse," in Chapter 47, *Trends in Psychiatric-Mental Health Care.*

Supportive Materials

MTI (producer): Epidemic (videocassette). 3710 Commerce Ave., Northbrook, IL 60062, Telaprograms, Inc.
(This 27-minute videocassette presents numerous vignettes depicting the problem of substance abuse among adolescents. Current and longer-term deleterious effects related to the problem are explored.)

FMS Production, Inc. (producer): Alcohol, Pills and Recovery (film). 1777 North Vine Street, Los Angeles, CA 90028, FMS Production, Inc.
(This 20-minute film narrated by Joseph Pursch, MD explores problems and rehabilitation issues associated with substance abuse.)

Chapter 27
Eating Disorders:
Anorexia Nervosa and Bulimia

Introduction

As stated by the author, the purpose of this chapter is to help the reader understand the etiology and dynamics of eating disorders and to utilize the nursing process effectively with anorexic and bulimic clients. Eating disorders challenge the nurse because of their complex psychosocial and physical problems.

Anorexia nervosa and bulimia are conditions that occur primarily, but not exclusively, among adolescent young women. The author presents descriptions of the anorexic and bulimic individual and the identifying clinical features of both. Etiologic factors are presented as a complex interaction of individual, family, and sociocultural factors. In applying the steps of the nursing process to clients with eating disorders, the author suggests the nurse apply the 11 functional health patterns to clients during the complex assessment phase. Specific questions to ask clients during the assessment are suggested and are very helpful. Various treatment modalities are discussed with their relative values, noting that family therapy has shown the most promise.

At the conclusion of Chapter 27, the author summarizes the following major points:

1. Anorexia nervosa and bulimia occur primarily among adolescent and young women.
2. Anorexia nervosa and bulimia have many etiologic factors in common and may be viewed as existing along a single spectrum of eating disorders.
3. Although multiple theories exist, most experts agree that eating disorders develop from a complex interaction of individual, family, and sociocultural factors.
4. Clients with eating disorders exhibit disturbances in many or all of the functional health patterns.
5. Treatment of clients with eating disorders occurs in both inpatient and outpatient settings and is a complex, and frequently lengthy, process.
6. Treatment approaches generally include a combination of individual psychotherapy, behavior modification, group therapy, and family therapy.
7. Desired client outcomes include normalization of weight and eating patterns, improved self-esteem, development of realistic thought processes, adaptive coping mechanisms, and constructive family processes.
8. Most clients require follow-up treatment to reinforce behavioral changes and prevent a return of disordered eating.

Key Terms

Anorexia nervosa
Bulimia
Model children
Enmeshment

Teaching Strategies

1. Have students think of an individual they knew, or know now, who may have had or has an eating disorder. Ask them to describe the individual's personality characteristics, family, behavior, and peer relations with regard to the psychodynamic, behavioral, sociocultural, and family systems theory presented in this chapter.
2. Practice/perform an assessment of a peer, utilizing the questions presented in the chapter's section on the 11 functional health patterns.
3. Discuss the statement "Behavior modification is useful to restore lost weight but inadequate to deal with psychological symptoms."
4. Delineate specific methodology for the interventions presented in this chapter's nursing care plan for clients with eating disorders.
5. Formulate an individualized nursing care plan for "Case Study: Julie" (contained in this chapter) at the point in time when the case study ended.
6. Identify the local, state, and national resources available to individuals (and their families) with eating disorders.

Part Six

Special Topics in Psychiatric-Mental Health Nursing

Chapter 28
The Emotionally Disturbed Child

Introduction

Chapter 28 addresses the problems and needs of emotionally disturbed children and their families, as well as the nurse's role in responding to the needs. At the outset of the chapter, the author addresses the undeniable prevalence of emotional disorders in children and suggests why precise statistics relative to the prevalence are lacking. Risk factors such as age, sex, culture, and family functioning, which are linked with the occurrence of childhood emotional disorders, are examined.

The author succinctly addresses numerous specific childhood emotional disorders. Cognitive, affective, and behavioral characteristics associated with the disorders are identified.

Use of the nursing process in relation to working with the emotionally disturbed child is examined. The author emphasizes the need for thorough assessment prior to planning and intervening. The reader is reminded that the child does not become disturbed in "a vacuum," and hence family involvement throughout all phases of applying the nursing process is of paramount importance. Numerous intervention methodologies are presented, as well as the need for ongoing evaluation.

At the conclusion of Chapter 28, the author summarizes the following major points:

1. The primary intervention in childhood emotional disorders is that of prevention.
2. Emotional disorders in children comprise a serious mental health problem in the United States, with estimates suggesting that at least one in ten children is in need of psychiatric-mental health services.
3. Many theories of childhood emotional disturbances postulate an interactive effect of genetic, biologic, physical, intrapsychic, familial, sociocultural, and environmental factors.
4. Assessment of emotional disorders of childhood requires an examination of both family functioning and the individual child.
5. Treatment planning is a collaborative activity involving the child, his family, and the mental health team.
6. Nursing intervention with the emotionally disturbed child requires maturity, thoughtfulness, and an ethical orientation to psychiatric-mental health care.

Key Terms

Adjustment disorders
Attention-deficit disorder
Conduct disorder

Phobia
Childhood depression
Infantile autism

Oppositional-defiance disorder
Anxiety disorders

Childhood-onset pervasive
developmental disorder
(childhood schizophrenia)
Childhood psychoses

Teaching Strategies

1. Have students observe children in a classroom setting on an inpatient child psychiatric unit or in an emotionally handicapped class of a public school *and* observe children in a mainstream classroom setting of a public school. Encourage students to focus their observations on one child as he or she relates to other children in the specific group. Have students report similarities and differences observed between children in these settings. Areas to assess may include the emotional assessment aspects included in the assessment section of Chapter 28.

2. Invite as guest lecturers a psychologist from a local school and a psychologist from a local child psychiatric inpatient unit. Have them share with students the background history, presenting problems, psychological test results, and treatment approaches used with several emotionally disturbed children with whom they have worked. Facilitate discussion of similarities and differences between data shared by the two lecturers. Encourage students to identify nursing implications, especially related to primary prevention.

3. Have students observe an "intake session," which includes the child and family and the mental health care team member, on a child inpatient or outpatient psychiatric unit. Using information presented in the assessment section of the Application of the Nursing Process to Emotionally Disturbed Children in Chapter 28, have students, as they observe, think about issues such as the following:
   a. How does the family define "the problem"?
   b. Who is the "spokesperson" for the family?
   c. Who seems most distressed by "the problem"?
   d. What do the parents hope the treatment team can do for them and their child?
   e. What is the general affect of the family? Of individuals in the family? Also, have students identify and discuss thoughts and feelings that they experienced during the session.

4. Have students read at least one book related to emotional disturbances in childhood. Examples of possible books include the following:

   Axline V: *Dibs in Search of Self*
   Rubin T: *Jordi, Lisa and David*
   Sechehayne M: *Autobiography of a Schizophrenic Girl*

   Have students identify cognitive, affective, and behavioral characteristics of the disorder and comment on interventions used in treatment.

5. Have students perform "The Mental Status Exam for a Child" contained in this chapter on a child known to them. Students should report to the group regarding:
   a. Thoughts, feelings, and observations about themselves during the exam
   b. Thoughts, feelings, and observations about the child during the exam

Supportive Materials

Light N: Group therapy with children. In Lego S (ed): The American Handbook of Psychiatric Nursing, pp 251–261. Philadelphia, JB Lippincott, 1984

Welt SR: Individual therapy with children. In Lego S (ed): The American Handbook of Psychiatric Nursing, pp 241–250. Philadelphia, JB Lippincott, 1984

Chapter 29
The Emotionally Disturbed Adolescent

Introduction

Adolescence is the pivotal age for individuals as they move through the developmental life span. Many myths abound about this crucial period, such as the one that states that rebelliousness is the typical path to autonomy. In order to demystify adolescence and to understand this period from a functional or dysfunctional frame of reference, the author of this chapter begins her discussion by presenting first a picture of normal adolescent development. Developmental categories focused on in this discussion are physical, sexual, emotional, and mental. The author then moves on to a presentation of adolescent disturbance by presenting various developmental theorists' (A. Freud, E. Erikson, H.S. Sullivan) views of adolescence, incidence, and causative theories. The dynamics of specific adolescent disturbances are described and discussed. Within this section, some of the more serious sociological problems involving adolescence are highlighted, such as runaway behavior, truant behavior, sexual acting out, adolescent pregnancy, substance abuse, depression and suicide, and delinquent behaviors.

The nursing process is applied to adolescent disorders. Throughout the chapter, the author consistently cautions the reader against portraying the adolescent in terms of a single image. Since the assessment of the adolescent is challenging because of the wide range of individual variation, the student is encouraged to assess the whole person and then make comparisons with normal limits in an age group. The adolescent should be included in the planning of professional intervention. The two goals of treatment with adolescents are to identify meanings of behavior and to work through conflicts that act as obstacles to success and happiness. The author stresses the need for the entire family to be incorporated into the treatment of an adolescent's problem. The psychotherapeutic interventions of any treatment modality used to assist adolescents in a treatment program focus on relationship building and reality testing. Finally, the author directs the nurse care-givers to heighten their vigilance in regard to their own feelings as they strive to help adolescents discover their own way.

At the conclusion of Chapter 29, the author summarizes the following major points:

1. The adolescent undergoes marked physical change, with individual differences within each sex almost as great as the differences between the sexes.
2. Sexual development proceeds by role-taking, which progresses toward sexual intimacy.
3. Emotional development includes defining or refining the self.
4. Mental development consolidates in the intellectual stage of formal operations for

many adolescents; moral development is evidenced as the adolescent moves through levels of conventional morality and postconventional or principled morality.

5. The incidence of adolescent emotional disorders is difficult to identify because of varying diagnostic biases.

6. Etiologic theories of adolescent disturbance examine the variables of family communication, childrearing style, personality, social pressures, and the sense of isolation.

7. In the assessment phase of the nursing process, the nurse gathers data about the adolescent's sense of identity, independence/dependence, self-image, strengths and talents, impulsivity, support systems, and sexuality.

8. In the nursing diagnosis phase, the nurse analyzes and categorizes client data and formulates nursing diagnoses.

9. In the planning stage, the nurse includes the adolescent and, hopefully, his family in decisions regarding outcomes of treatment based on assessed needs.

10. Various intervention strategies for working with disturbed adolescents may include family, group, individual, and milieu therapies, as well as behavior modification, psychopharmacology, limit setting, and communication skills.

11. The result of the evaluation phase may be to decide that the adolescent is ready for discharge from treatment or to decide to restart the nursing process with a fresh assessment of needs.

12. Working with adolescents is exciting and demanding and requires a firm awareness of self and a willingness to confront issues such as identification, separation, sexuality, and self-control.

Key Terms

Adolescent egocentrism
Good-boy–good-girl orientation
Law and order orientation
Social contract orientation
Value of human life orientation
Identity vs. self-diffusion
Communication within the family theory
Runaway behavior

Truant behavior
Problematic sexual behavior
Anorexia nervosa
Bulimia
Self-image
Body image
Self-concept
Self-awareness

Teaching Strategies

1. Have students discuss their opinions about the following myths of adolescent development, citing personal examples:
   a. Adolescence is a time of universal storm and stress.
   b. Rebelliousness is the typical pathway to autonomy.
   c. Peer-parent conflict is inevitable during adolescence.
   d. Peers replace parents as the major social influence in adolescence. Have students add any additional myths to this list based on their beliefs and experiences.

2. After completing exercise 1, have students discuss the validity or falsehood of the author's statement that it is critical that care-givers involved with disturbed

adolescents *not* portray them in terms of a single image.

3. If possible, and with written permission granted, have the student group seek out the following adolescent "types," and have them speak freely for 5 to 10 minutes on the significant memories of their adolescence. Tape their conversations.
   a. An unwed mother
   b. A sexually active male
   c. A sexually active female
   d. A class president, football star, prom queen, and so on
   e. An adolescent working at least 10 hours per week
   f. A minority male and female
   g. A white male and female
   h. An adolescent admitted to a psychiatric unit
   i. A homosexual or lesbian adolescent
   j. An adolescent not living with parents
   k. An adolescent in jail
   l. An adolescent prostitute
   m. An adolescent who has previously attempted suicide
   n. An anorexic adolescent
   o. A bulimic adolescent
   p. A gang member, female and male

   Have the student group listen to the tapes and discuss common themes, fears, and needs. Have students also focus on the differences and speculate on reasons for the variations, using one of the theoretical frameworks presented in the chapter.

4. Allow students opportunities to either observe or interact with individuals and groups of disturbed adolescents. Have students develop an assessment of one of the adolescents, focusing on (1) ego identity, (2) independent functioning, (3) self-image, (4) strengths, (5) impulsivity, (6) interpersonal relations, and (7) sexuality.

5. Have students observe and talk to nursing staff members on an adolescent unit and review care plans and nursing notes. Use the following questions to stimulate some of the discussion:
   a. What specific areas are focused on during the assessment? Are there definite criteria set up for each area assessed? Is an assessment tool used? What role does the nurse play in assessment?
   b. How is the adolescent involved in the decision making and goal setting relative to his care? How is the nurse involved?
   c. What part does the family play in the treatment plan? How is the nurse involved with families?
   d. What treatment modalities are used on the unit, and what are the roles, functions, and responsibilities of nursing personnel in each modality?
   e. What are the rules, expectations, and limits of the unit? What part does the nurse play in these?
   f. What protocols are used for discharge planning? How is the nurse involved?
   g. What therapeutic communication techniques are most used by nurses on the unit? Give examples of observed situations.
   h. How do the nurses evaluate the adolescent's progress toward attaining goals? What, why, when, and how are goals revised?

6. Have students write a mini-care plan using the following format:

Problem	Goals	Interventions	Evaluation
Identify a feeling that you anticipate being an obstacle to your being helpful to a disturbed adolescent.	How would you like to be different? In what way? *Criteria* How will you know if you have reached your goal?	Actions that you can take to assist you to reach your goals and meet your criteria.	Throughout your contact with disturbed adolescents, eview your goals (and specifically your criteria) in terms of your progress. Re-adjust goals, criteria, and interventions as necessary based on evaluation.

Supportive Materials

Dato C: Designing an adolescent inpatient and day program. In Lego S (ed): The American Handbook of Psychiatric Nursing, pp 134–143. Philadelphia, JB Lippincott, 1984

Dato C: Therapy with adolescents. In Lego S (ed): The American Handbook of Psychiatric Nursing, pp 262–273. Philadelphia, JB Lippincott, 1984

Hart N, Keidel G: The suicidal adolescent. Am J Nurs 80–84, 1979

Orvin G: Intensive treatment of the adolescent and his family. Arch Gen Psychiatry, 31:801–806, 1974

Chapter 30
Mental Retardation

Introduction

The author of Chapter 30 clearly states her personal goals and intent for writing about mental retardation. She hopes that discussion of the causes of mental retardation will strengthen nurses' efforts toward prevention. Additionally, she hopes to stimulate nursing interest in the field so that our discipline may become instrumental in demystifying the problems of mental retardation for the general public. The author points out that mental retardation is actually a constellation of symptoms, rather than a disease, and labeling is a serious and difficult responsibility because attaching labels may affect the care, treatment, and education of retarded persons. Specific standard tests employed to designate the label are described. Nurses are reminded that to work in the field of mental retardation, one must realize that, more often than not, retardation is only one of the impairments needing care and attention.

Advocacy is the keystone for Chapter 30. The author directs and implores nurses working in every area of human functioning to become involved. She speaks to the nursery nurse, the pediatric nurse, the public health nurse, the school nurse, and the politically adept nurse to be equipped to perform assessments, to discern disabilities, to be skilled and comfortable teaching and listening to families, to recognize risk factors, to assist families to find community resources, and to be interested in influencing legislation that affects retarded persons and their families.

At the conclusion of Chapter 30, the author summarizes the following major points:

1. Genetic factors may be chromosomal abnormalities such as errors in numbers of the chromosomes (nondisjunction) or errors in the structure of the chromosome due to breakage or translocation.
2. According to the laws of Mendelian inheritance, genetic disorders may be passed from generation to generation by traits found on the autosome or the sex chromosome in a dominant or recessive manner.
3. Acquired factors leading to mental retardation may occur prenatally, perinatally, or postnatally; these disorders may arise from trauma, disease, or infection of the mother during pregnancy or to the child following birth or from environmental problems such as malnutrition, lead poisoning, or child abuse.
4. Usually, those conditions more readily seen at birth causing multiple physical defects are the most difficult for parents.
5. Most mental retardation is mild in nature and is usually not diagnosed until some time after birth, when the child fails to develop academic skills.
6. The feelings ranging from guilt, depression, withdrawal, or rejection to denial or

anger are normal following the birth of a retarded child, and the nurse must communicate effectively with the parents to help them work through these feelings.

7. When the family has progressed past the crisis stage and is more accepting of intervention for the retarded child, referrals are made to find sources of parent teaching and infant stimulation.

8. Normalization, or social role volarization, as it is now called, is a widely accepted concept in the area of mental and physical disability that ensures that the client will not be segregated from the general population and made more deviant by lack of basic skills and appropriate dress and activities for age.

9. The nurse becomes an advocate for the client and the family by directing them to every resource that meets the needs of the client at each point in the life span and by providing nursing care that accents prevention, support, guidance, and teaching.

10. An advocate is also interested in the rights of the mentally retarded as a citizen, including becoming involved in the legislative process and in ethical issues that affect the client.

11. Knowledge and experience help the nurse to dispel old wives' tales and false beliefs that many people still hold and that continue to separate the retarded from the mainstream of society.

Key Terms

Mental retardation	Down's syndrome
Subaverage intellectual functioning	Turner's syndrome
Adaptive behavior	Polysomy of X
Mildly retarded	Klinefelter's syndrome
Moderately retarded	Mendelian inheritance
Severely retarded	Respite care
Profoundly retarded	

Teaching Strategies

1. Invite a school psychologist and student counselor to visit and discuss the following:
   a. Classification and testing of retarded students
   b. Resources available within the school system for the retarded student
   c. Anecdotes reflecting the success or failure of mainstreaming retarded students
   d. Peer acceptance or rejection
   e. Legal responsibilities of the school system to the retarded student

2. Have students research what the legal rights of retarded persons are in their state, as well as the programs for the retarded developed by their state.

3. Have students write two to three paragraphs responding to each of the questions posed by the author in the section "Ethical and Moral Issues." During class, read several of the responses to each question out loud to the group for further discussion, keeping the students names anonymous. Take as much time as possible for each question and responses.

4. Invite a group of parents of retarded persons to speak to your group. Include, if possible, parents who (1) gave the child up for adoption, (2) placed the child in an institution, and (3) chose to keep the child at home. (The local chapter of the

Association for Retarded Citizens should be a helpful contact.) Have the parents discuss the following question:

   a. How were you first told about your child's impairment? Who told you?
   b. How did the mother resolve the maternal tasks following the birth as discussed in the chapter?
   c. What were some of the influences on you that ended in the choice you made about placement of your child?
   d. Were the nurses helpful to you or not? How could they have been more helpful?
   e. What resources were helpful to you in making your decision?
   f. What is your relationship like now with your child? Your spouse? Your children?
   g. What would your child's siblings say about the choice that was made?

5. Discuss what the roles and responsibilities are for the postpartum nurse, the pediatric nurse, the office nurse, the school nurse, the public health nurse, and any other nurse in contact with retarded children and adults and their families, especially the mother.

6. Have students visit, if possible, a placement agency for the mentally retarded. Have students, as a group, discuss their observations using the suggestions by the author for assessing the child's environment.

7. Have students view and discuss the videotape Somebody Waiting, noted under Supportive Materials. This is an excellent tape (available for purchase) that shows the growth and enrichment potential for the staff caring for retarded people in a large institution, if and when staff personnel become interested and motivated.

8. Have students develop a list of resources available to themselves, retarded persons, and families of retarded persons, both within the hospital *and* in the community. Have students choose at least two of the resources and make personal visits. Discuss visits during group supervision.

9. Have students make a list of myths and facts regarding Down's syndrome children. Discuss the lists, especially in relation to the Hopkin's baby—a Down's syndrome infant who, on request by the parents, was not fed by the nurses for more than 20 days and who ultimately died.

10. Have copies of *Toward Independent Living* available for students to read and discuss in class. See the address for ordering this booklet within this chapter.

Supportive Materials

University of California Extension Media Center (producer): Somebody Waiting (Cassette recording #8441, VC1010). Berkeley, CA 94720.

Chapter 31
Organic Mental Disorders

Introduction

The classification of organic mental disorders previously has been thought primarily to be in the domain of those psychiatric-mental health personnel who deal with psychotic behavior. Today, the same morbid psychological phenomena have necessarily become the interest of a wider range of health care personnel. This is due to the fact that the origin of abnormal psychological or behavioral signs and symptoms also lies in an identified cerebral disease or dysfunction.

In organic mental disorders, the disturbed behavior is secondary to the brain's transient or permanent dysfunctioning or diseased state and is not a primary functional problem itself. Therefore, there are tremendous requirements of health care professionals in all clinical areas to correctly assess and diagnose the primary cause of behavior so that proper care and treatment can be provided. The patient population at risk for some organic mental disorders is varied, spanning all ages and including all forms of injuries, illnesses, and treatment modalities that may influence or insult the integrity of the brain.

The author presents causative factors and discusses their value in terms of determining the course of illness and ultimate prognosis. Various specific organic brain syndromes are described and categorized into one of the six main groups.

The author states that when the organic integrity of the brain is interrupted or interfered with, the result is maladaptive behavior, including deficits in the areas of sensorium, attention, orientation, perceptions, and memory capabilities. Descriptions of these deficits are included.

The author applies the nursing process to persons with organic mental disorders. She reminds the reader that the first step in determining treatment and nursing approaches is a clinical screening for any treatable physical causes of the problem. A list of typical screening tests is provided in chart form. Nurses are advised to use the person's family as the most reliable source of information as she attempts to break down the component parts of the person's behavior and assess how deficient each component is. Components discussed are intellect, level of consciousness, sensorium, needs for stimulation, attention span, perception, orientation, level of dependence, communication skills, and memory. In the planning stage of the nursing process, the reader is reminded of the necessity of family involvement. Plans of care should encourage family cohesiveness and stability. The intervention section suggests simple yet helpful activities for the nurse and, again, identifies the need to involve and support family members.

Because the needs of the person with an organic mental disorder, whether reversible or not, are so complex and involve both the physical and psychological realms, the author notes the physical and psychological drain experienced by nurses who care for persons with those disorders. Close evaluation of the relevance and outcome of interventions should decrease the nurses' often helpless and hopeless feelings.

At the conclusion of Chapter 31, the author summarizes the following major points:

1. The possible causes of organic mental disorders include primary brain disease, systemic disturbance, influences of exogenous substances, and withdrawal and residual effects of exogenous substances.
2. Aberrant behaviors associated with these disorders may include deficits in the areas of sensorium, attention, orientation perception, and memory.
3. Nonpredictable findings of organic mental disorders usually are associated with acute episodes, and the more predictable findings are associated with diseases that tend to be long term in nature.
4. Gathering and analyzing assessment data on a client with an organic mental disorder require participation of family members or friends who have been in close contact with the client.
5. Goal setting for the client with an organic disorder focuses on elimination of the organic cause, if possible, prevention of acceleration of the symptoms, and preservation of dignity.
6. Specific nursing interventions strive to maintain the client's optimal physical health, structure the environment, promote socialization and independent functioning, and preserve the family unit.
7. Hopefully, the nurse approaches the client with an organic mental disorder as a challenge to her professional skills.

Key Terms

Organic Mental Disorders: Senium
    Wernicke-Karsakoff's syndrome   Presenium
    Dementia   Sensorium
    Alzheimer's disease
    Pick's disease
    Multi-infarct dementia
    Huntington's chorea

Teaching Strategies

1. Have students define the terms *organic* and *functional*, *dementia* and *delerium*, *acute* and *chronic brain syndrome* and compare and contrast these definitions.
2. Invite a psychiatrist, a critical care nurse, an internist, a Ph.D. pharmacologist, and a neurologist to class and have them present case studies of various organic mental disorders arising from different causes.
3. Have students prepare at least three bibliography cards on various medications that can cause an organic brain syndrome. Have students refer to Table 31-1, Etiology of Organic Mental Disorders: Exogenous Substances, for suggestions.
4. If available, have students visit an Alzheimer's disease support group and write a short paper focusing on the student's thoughts and feelings prior to, during, and after the meeting.
5. Have students discuss the legal case of Mr. Roswell Gilbert, an elderly man in Florida who shot his wife who was ill with Alzheimer's disease. What would or

could they have done if they were he, instead of murdering his wife? What resources are available in your community to support the family members of persons with organic mental disorders?

6. Ask students to identify items and questions on their clinical assessment tool that would be helpful in assessing and diagnosing organic mental disorders.
7. Ask students to develop interventions for structuring the environment of an organic mental disordered hospitalized patient on their unit. Have them comment on the strengths and weaknesses of a critical care environment for these patients.

Supportive Materials

Burnside I: Nursing and the Aged, pp 148–163. New York, McGraw-Hill, 1976

Glaze B: One woman's story. J Gerontol Nurs 8:67–68, 1982

Gwyther L, Matteson M: Care for the caregivers. J Gerontol Nurs 9:92–95, 110, 1983

Hayter J: Helping families of patients with Alzheimer's disease. J Gerontol Nurs 8:81–86, 1982

LaPorte H: Reversible causes of dementia: A nursing challenge. J Gerontol Nurs 8:74–80, 1982

Chapter 32
Psychophysiologic Disorders

Introduction

Human beings are complex organisms composed of interrelated parts—psychosociological, biologic, and familial. Chapter 32 focuses on these parts and their impact on the choice to communicate psychophysiologically, as well as on the nurse's role in working with persons who are either prone to or are experiencing psychophysiologic disturbances.

No single factor is at the base of psychophysiologic responses. The author explores numerous possible psychosocial causative theories, including the psychoanalytic view, the psychodynamic view, life-experience perspective, and familial influences, as well as possible biologic causes. The chapter also focuses on feeling states and needs that may be communicated via physical illness.

The author differentiates between somatoform disorders and physical conditions that have an organic base. Also, in an effort to exemplify the holistic nature of humanity, the author examines physiologic disorders involving various body systems and accompanying psychosocial variables. Throughout the discussion of disorders such as peptic ulcer disease, anorexia nervosa, asthma, and essential hypertension, emphasis is given to the interrelationship of human psychosociological, biologic, and familial aspects. Similar emphasis occurs in the section of the chapter that addresses physiologic responses that frequently accompany depression and grief, loss, and change.

The nurse's role in primary, secondary, and tertiary prevention of psychophysiologic disorders is examined. The author uses the nursing process as the framework for discussing nursing care.

At the conclusion of Chapter 32, the author summarizes the following major points:

1. Humans are a composite of interrelated systems; hence, the mind and the body cannot be divorced from each other.
2. There is no single cause of psychophysiologic responses. Causative theories include psychosocial, biologic, and familial factors.
3. Physical illness may be a means of communicating feeling states and needs such as anxiety, anger, and dependency.
4. The integral relationship between a person's thinking, feeling, and physical status may be evident in physiologic disorders involving the gastrointestinal system and respiratory system, as well as in a person's response to depression and grief, loss, and change.
5. The nurse has a responsibility to participate in primary, secondary, and tertiary care aimed at preventing psychophysiologic disturbances.
6. During the primary prevention of psychophysiologic behavior, the nurse aims to promote functional family relationships and functional adaptation to life changes.

7. Most persons in need of secondary prevention for psychophysiologic disorders are nonpsychiatric patients.
8. Assessment, intervention, and evaluation for the psychophysiologically disturbed person focuses on physical and psychosocial life, as well as on the expressions of emotional needs and feelings.
9. The emotional themes of unmet dependency needs or unexpressed anger frequently underlie psychophysiologic behavior.
10. During the tertiary prevention of psychophysiologic behavior, the client's engagement in the process of change is the focus of nursing practice.

Key Terms

Psychosomatic
Somatoform disorder
La belle indifference
Psychological factors affecting physical conditions
Psychosomatic family

Teaching Strategies

1. During class, when discussing the common feelings and needs that persons may mask by psychophysiologic responses, offer students clinical examples of situations that they may encounter in nonpsychiatric settings. Examples may include the following:
   a. Mr. S., a patient with a diagnosis of myocardial infarction, refuses to acknowledge the seriousness of his condition. He refuses to remain in bed, and he continues to smoke. (The feeling experienced by Mr. S. is anxiety. He defends against this feeling by using the unconscious defense mechanism of denial. Consciously, he believes that nothing is wrong with his heart because he cannot deal with the fright of disability and possible death that recognizing the truth would entail.)
   b. Mrs. J., an ambulatory patient with ulcerative colitis, frequently rings the call bell shortly after the nurse has been in her room. Her requests include such things as wanting more ice in her pitcher, wanting an extra blanket, and wanting someone to sharpen the picture on the television. (Mrs. J. is possibly unable to express dependency needs and needs for affection in a functional way. Being hospitalized may well intensify Mrs. J.'s dependency needs, and she defends against the anxiety by indirectly communicating them.)
   Have students identify nursing interventions that would be helpful for these patients.
2. Encourage students to share thoughts and feelings evoked by situations similar to those suggested above. Have students describe how their thoughts and feelings might impact on their delivery of care. If they deem that there would be a negative impact, what resources would they use to help them with their reaction?
3. Encourage students to share ways in which they perceive themselves responding psychophysiologically. Have students speculate about possible meanings behind their behavior.
4. Have students complete the social readjustment rating scale included in Chapter 32.

What did they learn about themselves? How might this information be used by them?

5. Invite as a guest lecturer a liaison nurse from a local hospital. Have the nurse share with students clinical examples that illustrate theory discussed in Chapter 32.

Supportive Materials

Boyle MP, Koff E, Gudas LJ: Assessment and management of anorexia nervosa. Matern Child Nurs J 6:412–418, 1981

Whitney FW: How to work with a crock. Am J Nurs 87–91, 1981

Part Seven

Crisis

Chapter 33
Crisis Theory and Intervention

Introduction

Whether or not persons find themselves in crisis does not depend on the stressors in life, but on the person's possession of and capacity to use coping abilities sufficient to adaptively deal with these stressors. The paradox of crisis lies in the severity of insult to the person's functioning (the danger) and the possibility of dealing with the insults, with assistance, to the degree that the individual is, indeed, stronger after the crisis (adaptive opportunity). The final resolution of crisis for a person therefore has both frightening and gratifying aspects for both the client and the health care provider.

The reader is reminded that intervention during crisis has been found to greatly reduce the incidence and severity of mental disorders. Therefore, it is incumbent on all psychiatric-mental health nurses to have both an understanding of crisis development and the interpersonal skills by which to prevent and resolve crises. Chapter 33 assists the reader in these goals. A crisis is described from theoretical and operational points of view. This discussion is helpful in that it focuses the nurse on aspects of a crisis that have implications for primary, secondary, and tertiary treatment programs. Critical differences in crisis therapy from more traditional therapies are noted, as well as behavioral characteristics necessary for the nurse therapist.

In the section applying the nursing process to crisis intervention, assessment and analysis are noted to be the most critical and time–consuming steps. The nurse's appropriate assessment is highly significant to the entire treatment approach chosen. The client's feelings, perceptions of the crisis event, support systems, coping skills, and suicidal thoughts are the areas noted as deserving intensive inspection during assessment. It is essential to planning that the nurse actually involve the client and significant others. The goals of crisis intervention are different from those of other therapies. The author focuses on the need of the intervener to solve the immediate problem. Therapeutic interventions during crisis intervention are highlighted. Common communication techniques are used, but the interviewer takes a much more assertive and initiating role because of the time limitations and goals of therapy. Variations of concepts and interventions related to crisis work with families are also included in this chapter.

At the conclusion of Chapter 33, the author summarizes the following major points:

1. Crisis theory evolved from the study of grief and bereavement by many researchers.
2. Persons who are faced with an overwhelming threat try their usual coping mechanisms and, if they are unsuccessful in solving the problem, experience a mounting level of anxiety.
3. A crisis occurs when persons are unable to solve a problem that they perceive as overwhelming, when the usual coping mechanisms fail to solve the problem, when

their perception of the event is distorted, and when they lack the necessary social support.

4. People experiencing a crisis are more open to learning new coping skills to deal with their problems.

5. There exists the potential for a person in crisis to develop more adaptive coping and, therefore, healthier functioning capabilities after the crisis experience.

6. Maturational crises result from developmental changes and milestones, such as puberty, marriage, old age, and death of a loved one.

7. Situational crises result from sudden, unexpected events, such as divorce, illness, injury, and loss of a job.

8. Crisis intervention is a thinking, directive, problem-solving approach that focuses only on the client's immediate problems.

9. Nurses are often the first health care professionals in contact with the client in crisis and, therefore, are in a unique position to intervene in crises.

10. Any crisis intervener needs a colleague or supervisor with whom to discuss feelings and plan approaches and from whom to receive support and encouragement.

Key Terms

Crisis

Phases of a crisis

Maturational crisis

Situational crisis

Crisis intervention

Crisis team approach

Teaching Strategies

1. Have students describe the most stressful event in their lives and assess their feelings, perception of the event, support systems, coping skills, and potential for self-harm during the events. Ask them to discuss their thoughts about why this stress did *not* result in a crisis. (Students may be referred to the Holmes-Rahe social readjustment rating scale. See first entry under Supportive Materials.)

2. Focusing on the phases of a crisis, have the students answer the following questions:
   a. At what phase is a person most ready and accepting of intervention?
   b. What are some primary prevention interventions useful for averting a crisis?
   c. What resources are available to people at each phase of crisis development in your community?

3. Discuss thoughts about the observation many people make that one of the differences between maturational and situational crises is that there seems to be higher levels of anxiety associated with maturational crises.

4. Discuss categories of medications that are, and are not, used during outpatient crisis intervention. Give the rationale for the limited use of medications in crisis interventions.

5. Have students observe at a crisis group, a crisis intervention program, or a hot-line service. Discuss as a group the observations made, using the major concepts discussed in Chapter 33.

6. During a supervision group, create a poster having two columns that points out the major differences between crisis intervention therapy and crisis intervener communication techniques and traditional therapy and basic therapeutic interpersonal

techniques. "The Therapeutic Dialogue: The Client in Crisis" in this chapter may stimulate beginning discussion.

7. Have students read the case study at the end of the chapter, J. L., and during class discuss the questions listed.

Supportive Materials

Holmes TH, Rahe RH: The social readjustment rating scale. Psychosom Res 11:213–218, 1967

Neville D, Barnes S: The suicidal phone call. J Psychosoc Nurs Ment Health Serv 23:14–18, 1985

Schneidman ES, Farberow NL: Clues to Suicide. New York, McGraw–Hill, 1957

Swanson A: Crisis intervention. In Lego S (ed): The American Handbook of Psychiatric Nursing, pp 235–240. Philadelphia, JB Lippincott, 1984

Chapter 34
Rape and Sexual Assault

Introduction

No one in our society is immune from the impact that the violent crime of rape has on the human condition. The victim, significant others, and people who perhaps merely hear of the event are confronted with facing their fears of vulnerability, loss of control, perversion, bodily harm, and death. Nurses can play a significant role in helping people "become strong in the broken places" following a rape experience.

In Chapter 34, the author defines rape and sexual assault and explores pertinent historical, legal, psychological, and sociological perspectives of these crimes. Types of sexual assault that include the blitz rape, the confidence rape, accessory-to-sex with inability to consent, and the sex-stress situation are described. Myths about rape and attitudes about "who is to blame" are identified.

The question of who rapes and why is answered in the section pertaining to character-istics of rapists. The author points out that "rapists perform sexual acts in the service of nonsexual needs." Types of rapists described include the power rapist, the angry rapist, and the sadistic rapist. Detecting the underlying need of the rapist has treatment implications for the victim and the offender.

The author succinctly describes the adaptive nature of the *rape trauma syndrome*. During this mending process, the victim works to overcome feelings of vulnerability, fright, and helplessness and to regain control and equilibrium. The phases of this process range from the acute phase of disorganization to reorganization and recovery. The author highlights impediments as well as assistive maneuvers that impact on the victim's ability or willingness to recover from rape trauma.

The nursing process framework is used to discuss the nurse's role in assisting victims of rape and sexual assault. In assessment and formulation of nursing diagnoses, the nurse must attend to the physical and emotional status of the victim. Common emotional concerns of victims are identified in this section. When setting goals, the immediate, interim, and long-range phases of the rape trauma syndrome guide the nurse's plans. During the intervention phase, establishment of a nonthreatening therapeutic alliance that facilitates open expression of thoughts and feelings by the victim is of paramount importance. Immediate intervention also focuses on the nurse's taking initiative in preparing the victim for medical and legal examination, as well as exploring physical safety concerns of the victim and supportively coaching significant others. Written and verbal instructions regarding follow-up medical treatment and the availability of supportive counseling are given to the victim during the first contact as a means of assisting her during reorganization and ultimate recovery.

At the conclusion of Chapter 34, the author summarizes the following major points:

1. Theoretical perspectives of rape and sexual assault include historical references, legal definitions, psychological reactions, and sociological views as means of

examining types of assaults and characteristics of assailants.

2. Rape trauma syndrome is the process of adaptation experienced by the victim of rape as she strives to overcome her feelings of vulnerability, fear, and helplessness and regain her equilibrium. It can be viewed as a posttraumatic syndrome.

3. Unresolved sexual trauma and silent reaction to rape delay or inhibit a woman's recovery from rape crisis.

4. Community intervention programs encompass the medical, legal, police, and judicial institutions with which the victim of rape or sexual assault must interact.

5. Nursing assessment of the victim of rape or sexual assault focuses on the woman's physical and emotional state, concerns for physical safety, anxiety about significant others, perception of the event, coping skills, and the availability of people supportive to her.

6. Planning for the victim who has just been assaulted includes medical attention and the provision of physical safety for her. Intermediate and long-range planning consists of continued contact with the victim, supportive counseling, and helping her reorganize her life.

7. Nursing intervention for the victim of rape or sexual assault aims to develop a therapeutic alliance that will help her begin to ventilate her feelings and explore what life changes she wishes to make.

8. Preparation for medical events, police investigations, and court proceedings help demystify these procedures for the woman.

9. Anticipatory guidance is necessary for the family and friends of the rape victim to help them explore their own feelings and identify ways to become more supportive of her.

10. Follow-up plans for medical appointments and supportive counseling help the victim reintegrate and reorganize her life.

11. To enhance their therapeutic potential, nurses must recognize and face their own fears and stereotypical views of rape and sexual assault.

Key Terms

Rape
Sexual assault
Types of sexual assault:
    Blitz rape
    Confidence rape
    Accessory-to-sex
    Sex-stress situation
Types of rapists:
    Power rapist
    Anger rapist
    Sadistic rapist
    Date rapist

Rape crisis
Rape trauma syndrome:
    Disorganization phase
    Reorganization
Unresolved sexual trauma

Teaching Strategies

1. Elaborate in class on the common myths and facts about rape. Share the myth, have students refute the myth with what they believe is the fact, and then share the actual fact with them. (The second and third references under Supportive Materials may

be useful in organizing this strategy.)

2. Have students determine what community resources (medical, legal, police, and judicial) are available to rape victims. Have students interview key people linked with the various resources about the assistance that they offer to victims. Have them present their findings to the class.

3. Have the students complete unfinished sentences such as the following:
    a. Rape is _____.
    b. My idea of the typical rapist is _____.
    c. My idea of the typical rape victim is _____.
    d. The penalty for rape should be _____.
    e. The person who is to blame for rape occurring is _____
    _____.
    f. Women who are raped feel like _____.
    g. The rapist feels like _____.
    h. A man who has been dating the same woman for 6 months can _____.
    i. A man who has had sexual relations with a woman many times has a right to expect _____.
    j. Women who dress seductively are _____.
    k. A woman who is on the street late at night by herself is _____
    _____.
    l. The thought of being raped _____
    _____.
    m Society expresses revulsion about rape because _____
    _____.
    n. A known rapist is admitted for an appendectomy to the unit where I work. I am assigned to be his primary nurse. I feel _____
    because _____.

4. Invite as a guest lecturer a representative from the National Organization for Women (NOW) to speak with the class about past and current efforts by NOW to influence legislative changes that support victims of rape and sexual assault. Have this person share the current legislation in your locale.

5. Have students discuss their thoughts and feelings about blitz rape, confidence rape, accessory-to-sex with inability to consent, and the sex-stress situation described in Chapter 34. What are the similarities and differences between their thoughts and feelings associated with these crimes?

Supportive Materials

Adams C, Fay J: Nobody told me it was rape: A parent's guide for talking with teen-agers about acquaintance rape and sexual exploitation. (This guide is available only by phone or mail order from Network Publications, 1700 Mission Street, Santa Cruz, CA (404) 429-9822.)

Foley T: The client who has been raped. In Lego S (ed): The American Handbook of Psychiatric Nursing, pp 475–491. Philadelphia, JB Lippincott, 1984

Foley T: Counseling the victim of rape. In Stuart G and Sundeen S (eds): Principles and Practice of Psychiatric Nursing, pp 840–842. St. Louis, CV Mosby, 1983

Chapter 35
Violence within the Family

Introduction

Chapter 35 examines the specific areas of child, elder, and spouse abuse as types of violence occurring within some families. Physical and behavioral indicators of children who are victims of physical, sexual or emotional abuse or neglect are presented. Wife battering is also described.

The author emphasizes the many problems associated with reporting and accurately documenting the incidence of the significant problem of abuse. All states currently have a mandatory reporting law for child abuse; however, legal protection for abused spouses and elders is less formalized.

A multidisciplinary theoretical approach to the reasons for violence and abuse in some families is offered. Authorities representing such disciplines as psychology, sociology, physiology, and biology express their thoughts.

Common characteristics of abusing parents, spouses, and children of elders are identified. For example, abusing parents who engage in uncontrolled battering have been characterized as having particular personality deficits (*e.g.*, the psychotic personality, the inadequate personality, the passive-aggressive personality, and the sadistic personality). Aside from personality variables that may characterize either the perpetrators or victims of abuse, the author emphasizes that the individual reactions to certain stressors such as financial crises, physical ills, and drug dependence play a crucial role in abusive situations.

No one in a violent family system is spared from the negative impact of the experience. Victims frequently bear reversible or irreversible physical damage, as well as behavioral and emotional maladies. Similarly, family members who are not directly victimized may, in fact, experience emotional and behavior problems such as depression and truancy. Learning a cycle of violence that tends to repeat in future generations is yet another tragedy associated with living in a violent family system.

Since nurses work in a variety of clinical settings, they are in a unique position to detect and respond to abuse within families. The author delineates numerous specific behavioral predictors of potential or actual child abuse, as well as factors that actually assist with the diagnosis. Cues to detecting and diagnosing spouse abuse and elder abuse are also offered. Planning care and setting goals with victims and perpetrators of abuse mandates that the nurse suspend judgments and facilitate a trusting environment. To do this, nurses need to be aware of, accepting of, and willing to work through, their own feelings, especially anger, which are apt to surface. The author emphasizes nursing interventions that are directed toward the victim, the perpetrator, and the entire family.

At the conclusion of Chapter 35, the author summarizes the following major points:

1. The six specific types of abuse recognized by Parents Anonymous are physical

abuse, physical neglect, emotional abuse, emotional neglect, sexual abuse, and verbal abuse.

2. Physical abuse is more empirically observable than emotional abuse and, therefore, predominates the available literature on family violence; however, physical abuse may be the least frequently occurring form of abuse within the family.

3. Emotional maltreatment and sexual abuse are probably more common than major physical trauma to children.

4. The incidence, significance, and impact of all forms of family violence are tremendous.

5. There exist several decades of multidisciplinary work on the development of theories and the application of these theories to the issue of violence, in general, and family violence, in particular.

6. Although early research on the causes of family abuse emphasized the personality deficits of abusers, more recent studies have focused on the factors of financial stress, drug dependency, marital discord, and others.

7. The nurse must recognize the characteristics of abusing families and the impact of abuse on the entire family, rather than limit attention to the individual victim.

8. Nursing assessment of the battered child includes the identification of the predictors of abuse and vulnerable infants, physical and psychosocial information about the child, and specific data about the injury.

9. Assessment of the battered woman often reveals a history of repeated injuries, psychosomatic complaints, and drug and alcohol abuse.

10. Awareness of the possibility of elder abuse has been slim due to limited respect society gives to the elderly.

11. It is difficult for the health care professional to document abuse within families.

12. The goals and principles of intervening with the abused victim and family focus on an accepting, objective, and nonjudgmental approach to the family.

13. Health care providers must be familiar with the available community resources and their usefulness to the client and family.

14. Because child abuse, wife abuse, and elder abuse often occur together in a family unit, the nurse or other health care professional may need to intervene on behalf of more than one family member.

15. The nurse must become aware of, and face, her own feelings in response to working with the violent family.

16. Nurses need to become involved in the area of social change through consciousness raising, community education, and the legal process.

Key Terms

Physical abuse
Physical neglect
Emotional abuse
Emotional neglect
Sexual abuse
Verbal abuse
Domestic violence
Elder abuse

Adolescent maltreatment
Parents Anonymous
Stages of the abuse cycle:
    Tension buildup
    Acute
    Reconciliation

Teaching Strategies

1. In an effort to help students become more aware of their thoughts and feelings about abuse, have them complete unfinished sentences such as the following:
   a. Parents who abuse or neglect children are _____.
   b. Abusive parents deserve to be _____
      because _____.
   c. I feel _____ toward abusive parents.
   d. I feel _____ toward the abused child.
   e. If I cared for an abused hospitalized child, I would respond to the parents like
      _____.
   f. The best way to handle an abused child is _____
      _____.
   g. Women who remain in a battering situation are _____
      _____.
   h. I feel _____ toward men who batter.
   i. Elder abuse is _____ because
      _____.
   j. Women who abuse their spouses are _____.

2. Either have students ascertain state legislation that protects the child from abuse or present the legislation in class. Also, delineate the local procedure for reporting child abuse or neglect.

3. Share with students data that illustrate the significance of child, spouse, or elder abuse or neglect in their locale. These data may be obtained from the Department of Social Services (DSS) and may include information about areas such as the following:
   a. Within the past year, how many abuse cases did the DSS have on record?
   b. Out of the number of abuse cases on record, how many were for physical abuse or neglect and how many were for sexual abuse?
   c. How do statistics for the local county compare with those of other counties in the state?
   d. What size abuse or neglect caseload does a DSS worker carry?
   e. What are the responsibilities of the caseworker?

4. Have students determine available community resources for victims and perpetrators of child, spouse, and elder abuse. If possible, have students visit these resources.

5. In an effort to help students appreciate and think about the generational cyclic nature of abuse, which the author in Chapter 35 addresses, present the schematic "World of Abnormal Rearing," which is included in K. Scharer's article entitled "Nursing Therapy with Abusive and Neglectful Families" (see Supportive Materials).

6. Facilitate student responses to the discussion questions posed at the conclusion of "Case Study—Maria, a Battered Wife," which is included in Chapter 35.

7. Have students role-play assessment interviewing sessions with an abused child, an abused elder, a battered woman, a perpetrator of child abuse, a perpetrator of spouse abuse, and a perpetrator of elderly abuse. Aside from suggested assessment factors included in Chapter 35, J. Campbell and J. Humphreys's book, *Nursing Care of Victims of Family Violence*, may assist students in conducting the interview (see

Supportive Materials).

8. Have students call the following hotlines for information: Child Abuse: (800) 422-4453, Parent's Anonymous: (800) 421-0353

Supportive Materials

Campbell J, Humphreys J: Nursing Care of Victims of Family Violence. Reston, Va, Reston Publishing, 1984

Hunka C, O'Toole R: Self-help therapy in Parents Anonymous. J Psychosoc Nurs Ment Health Serv 23:24–32, 1985

Nikstaitis G: Therapy for men who batter. J Psychosoc Nurs Ment Health Serv 23:33–36, 1985

Scharer K: Nursing therapy with abusive and neglectful families. J Psychosoc Nurs Ment Health Serv 12–21, September 1979

Chapter 36
Crisis of Perinatal Loss and Depression

Introduction

This chapter begins with a discussion on depression as a psychological disturbance occurring at times in the postnatal period. Mental health problems such as maternity blues, postpartum depression, and postpartum psychosis are described and discussed. The main focus of the chapter, however, is an exploration of the topic of perinatal loss and its effect on the client and her family. The application of the nursing process to the client with perinatal loss is described. In discussing the assessment phase of the client, the author uses grief and mourning frameworks identified by Lindemann and Kübler-Ross. There is also a discussion of individual differences in grieving among mother, father, siblings, and other family members. Examples of nursing diagnoses are suggested. Finally, the author reminds the reader that the grief responses of the care-givers are significant, often similar to those experienced by the bereaved parents, and require the same consideration as that provided for the client/family.

At the conclusion of Chapter 36, the author summarizes the following major points:

1. Perinatal loss can create a situational crisis in addition to the existing maturational crisis of pregnancy.
2. There exists a difference of opinion as to whether depression during the postnatal period is a distinct entity.
3. The DSM III-R includes depression in the postpartal period with classifications of other major psychotic disorders.
4. The client and family with a perinatal loss must progress through the normal grief and mourning stages.
5. The assessment of a client and her family experiencing the death of a baby may include normal symptoms and behaviors of grief and indicators of potential pathologic bereavement.
6. Specific short- and long-term goals are formulated for the client and family in order to facilitate the accomplishment of each stage of the mourning process.
7. Intervention strategies are designed to promote the concept of attachment and detachment in the resolution of the mourning process.
8. Evaluation of the specific perinatal grief crisis interventions determines whether projected client outcomes have been achieved.
9. Because o the difficult nature of working with parents who have experienced a perinatal death, the nurse must have adequate and available support and encouragement.

Key Terms

Maternity blues
Postpartum depression
Postpartum psychosis
Attachment process
Incongruent grieving

Teaching Strategies

1. Have students review and present cases of psychiatric admissions for maternity blues, postpartum depression, or postpartum psychosis.
2. Have students identify, discuss, and visit (if possible) local support groups for individuals/families who have experienced perinatal loss.
3. Have student groups develop a bibliography for individuals/families who have experienced perinatal loss that includes books and articles for the mother, father, siblings, and other family members.
4. Have students identify the major aspects of discharge planning for individuals/families who have experienced perinatal loss. What resources are available to the nurse prior to discharge? After discharge?
5. Have students read "Losing a Baby," continued in this chapter. Identify what verbal *and* nonverbal behaviors of the nurse could have been more helpful. Identify what physical *and* psychological behaviors would have been helpful. Discuss potential reasons for the nurse's nonhelpful behaviors. React to this statement by a patient, "A nurse can be a wonderful, comforting distraction for a grieving patient."
6. Have students read "Case Study: Planning Care for the Client Who Has Experienced a Perinatal Loss (stillbirth)," contained in this chapter. List those nursing interventions which facilitate the concepts of attachment and detachment.
7. Have students develop a nursing care plan for the nurse(s) who has cared for an individual/family who experienced perinatal loss.

Supportive Materials

Carr D, Knupp S: Grief and perinatal loss: A community hospital approach to support. JOGN, 130–139, 1985
Coddington C: Perinatal death: Aiding grief resolution. US Navy Med 19–21, 1983
Cordell AS, Apolito R: Family support in infant death. JOGN 10: 281–285, 1981
Benfield DG, Leib S, Vollman J: Grief response of parents to neonatal death and parent participation in deciding care. Pediatr Med 52(1):171–177, 1978

Chapter 37
Suicide

Introduction

The author states that the purpose of this chapter is to help the reader understand the nature of suicidal behavior and to assess and care for persons at risk for suicide. Although suicidal behavior appears in all age groups, the likelihood of successful suicide increases with age. There are many postulated viewpoints and theories about the cause of suicide, none of which proves a singular causal explanation for all cases. The author discusses influences such as depression, social trends, intrapsychic drives and desires, and interpersonal crises. The dynamics of suicide are described in terms of the act's being a sort of message, and the meaning of the message is unique to each individual. Escapist, aggressive, oblative, and lucid suicides represent categories of possible messages.

In applying the nursing process to suicide, the author notes that assessment is the key to the care of the suicidal client. Suicidal risk is evaluated amidst a complex set of behaviors and thoughts. Direct and indirect verbal and nonverbal clues to suicide are presented in chart form. The author notes that a change in expected patterns of behavior is often the most important indicator of suicide risk. The goals of the assessment are to establish a likelihood of self-harm, understand the meaning of the behavior, and begin a therapeutic alliance with the patient that will decrease the need to communicate through self-destructive behaviors. The author notes that it is imperative for the nurse to include family and friends in data gathering in order to either identify the precipitants to the suicidal act or identify clues within behavioral patterns.

A major aspect of any plan of care for a suicidal patient is balance. The balance is between offering sufficient provisions of safety and protection while allowing enough freedom and autonomy in which the patient can move to use those available resources necessary for growth and change. The author describes and discusses specific resources and interventions for suicidal persons who are either in the community or in a hospital setting.

At the conclusion of Chapter 37, the author summarizes the following major points:

1. Suicide occurs as a response to life situations in an intrapersonal or interpersonal context.
2. Although some evidence suggests a biochemical basis for suicidal behavior, the most commonly held etiologic theories define suicide as the result of an interpersonal or intrapsychic crisis.
3. The suicidal person experiences feelings of ambivalence, anger, isolation, and desperation.
4. The suicide act has many meanings and serves to communicate a dramatic message to others.
5. The nurse uses the nursing process to determine the degree of suicide risk of an individual and to discover the message expressed through the suicidal behavior.

6. In assessment, the nurse examines six factors: the presence of clues to suicide, the means by which the person sought help, the suicidal plan, the person's mental state, his support systems, and his life-style.

7. Nursing care is planned in conjunction with the suicidal individual and other resource personnel, including psychiatric staff and the client's significant others.

8. Nursing interventions, based on the degree of suicidal risk of the client, focus on providing safety and establishing a therapeutic alliance.

9. One goal of nursing care is to help the client express his unique message.

10. The nurse uses dyadic skills to help the client learn less destructive means to cope with stressors.

11. Nursing intervention continues after a completed suicide through activities with the "survivor-victims" of the suicide.

12. Evaluation of nursing care is based on two questions: Were the clues identified early enough to permit intervention? Was the intervention appropriate and effective?

13. Nurses and other psychiatric-mental health care providers need opportunities to express their feelings of anger and frustration at the behaviors of suicidal clients and to work through these feelings to achieve objectivity and empathy.

Key Terms

Suicide:
    Anomic
    Egoistic
    Altruistic
    Partial
    Escapist suicide
    Aggressive suicide
    Oblative suicide
    Lucid suicide

No suicide contract
Resuscitation stage
Rehabilitation stage
Renewal stage
Psychological autopsy

Teachng Strategies

1. Have students visit a hot-line or suicide prevention service in your community to find out information about the following:
   a. Number of calls a day/month related to suicide
   b. Demographic information related to suicide calls
   c. Therapeutic interventions used by counselors
   d. Community resources available for referral

2. In order to assess the student's values, beliefs, and attitudes toward self-destructive behaviors, have them answer and discuss the following questions in terms of how their responses may or may not be helpful to them in assisting suicidal patients and families:
   a. Is suicide ever justifiable?
   b. Are people who attempt suicide with nonlethal methods trying to get attention?
   c. Are all suicides preventable?
   d. Are all persons who attempt or commit suicide psychiatrically ill?
   e. Is it possible that you (student) could become suicidal?
   f. Do movies, records, and so on influence people to attempt suicide?

3. Have students respond to the following myths about suicide with factual information they have gathered through their reading:
   a. Individuals who verbalize suicidal thoughts do not actually follow through with attempts.
   b. Suicide is an impulsive action on the part of an individual.
   c. Suicidal individuals are completely intent on dying.
   d. Persons remain suicidal throughout life.
   e. "Improvement" of depressive states is an indication that the danger of suicide has passed.
   f. Suicides selectively affect certain economic and occupational classes.
   g. Suicidal individuals are psychiatrically ill.
   h. Suicidal tendencies are hereditary.
4. In order to desensitize students to the direct interviewing techniques used to assess suicidal risk, have the students role-play interviewing suicidal patients using the following questions.
   a. Are you so upset that you are thinking of killing yourself? Are you thinking of hurting yourself?
   b. What are you thinking of doing? Have you thought about ways to kill yourself?
   c. Do you have a gun? Do you know how to use it? Do you have ammunition? Do you have pills? Where are the pills? How do you plan to get the pills? The gun?
   d. What time of the day or night do you plan to do this? Is there anyone else around during this time?
5. Discuss what resources are available to the nurse in the community who is working with a person who she believes is a high suicide risk and is in need of hospitalization but who refuses to be hospitalized.
6. Discuss the psychiatric commitment procedure and requirements in your state.
7. Have students develop a 24-hour plan of care on a psychiatric unit for a highly suicidal patient. Particularly focus on those nursing behaviors that seek to balance the safety and security of the patient while at the same time providing enough freedom and autonomy. Include in the discussion (1) the "no-suicide" contract, (2) protocols for giving medications, change of shift supervision, close observation or 1:1 supervision, and (3) participation in unit and off-unit activities.
8. Have students identify and visit at least one community agency that serves as a resource/support agency for the survivor-victims of a suicide. Share experiences with the group.

Supportive Materials

Assey J: The suicide prevention contract. Perspect Psychiatr Care 23:99–103, 1985

Barile L: The client who is suicidal. In Lego S (ed): The American Handbook of Psychiatric Nursing, pp 398–403. Philadelphia, JB Lippincott, 1984

Cochran P (producer): Suicide: Causes and Prevention (slides and audiotape). Pleasantville, NY, Ibis Media, 1976

Hipple J, Cimbolic P: The Counselor and Suicidal Crisis. Springfield, Ill, Charles C Thomas, 1979

Webster M: Assessing suicide potential. In Lego S (ed): The American Handbook of Psychiatric Nursing, pp 28–33. Philadelphia, JB Lippincott, 1984

Zillman, MA: Suicide precautions. In Lego S (ed): The American Handbook of Psychiatric Nursing, pp 528–529. Philadelphia, JB Lippincott, 1984

Part Eight

Community Care from Crisis to Long -Term Intervention

Chapter 38
Community Mental Health

Introduction

Chapter 38 presents a succinct overview of the history of community mental health in the United States, as well as the present status and future possibilities of community mental health care in this country. The chapter stresses that the target of care in community mental health is the community as the client or the client in interaction with his environment. Active involvement by the client in his treatment is presented as a basic tenet of community mental health.

Primary, secondary, and tertiary prevention are focused on as the goals of community mental health care. Examples of each type of prevention are offered and illustrate the comprehensive nature of community mental health care. Provision of these services in the immediate community of the client is stressed.

In addition, Chapter 38 elaborates on the nurse's role in delivering community mental health care. The student is exposed to the nursing process as it applies to community mental health.

At the conclusion of Chapter 38, the author summarizes the following major points:

1. Numerous historical events interface with community mental health development in the United States. Currently, communities within our country face a multitude of challenges as they strive to maintain the availability of community mental health to their citizens.
2. Community mental health services are designed to provide comprehensive, continuous care to the people who need it.
3. The aims of community mental health are the prevention of illness/disorder (primary prevention), limitation of disability (secondary prevention), and rehabilitation (tertiary care).
4. Mental health workers, professional and paraprofessional, are used in addition to psychiatrists to provide mental health care to individuals, families, and communities.
5. The shift in funding from the federal to state level has reduced mental health services and endangered the viability of community mental health.
6. The community mental health nurse applies the nursing process (assessment and analysis, planning, intervention, and evaluation) to provide comprehensive services to clients.

Key Terms

Community mental health
Community mental health care
Primary prevention
Secondary prevention
Tertiary prevention
Community Mental Health Centers Act
Community mental health nurse's role
Nursing process as it relates to community mental health nursing

Teaching Strategies

1. Have the students visit at least one community mental health agency during the course in which this content is presented. Either require a written or verbal report of the experience, preferably verbal, so that other students benefit from all experiences. During the visit and in the report, the student may meet objectives such as the following:
   a. Identify the goals, purposes, and functions of the agency.
   b. Identify what population the agency serves.
   c. Identify how a nurse might refer a client to the agency.
   d. Identify the strengths and limitations of the agency.
   e. Identify nursing's role within the agency.
2. Use community mental health agencies as clinical placement sites. Assist students to meet course objectives in these settings.
3. Assist students to increase their exposure to community mental health in their community by inviting as guest lecturers persons within the community who are involved in community mental health. Organize a panel presentation delivered by persons representing mental health perspectives from the local/state government, the local/state board of mental health, individual community resources (hot-line, crisis intervention centers, substance abuse commissions, parents anonymous, inpatient units.
4. Have students interview five individuals of their choosing, and query them regarding issues such as the following:
   a. What do you think of the availability of community mental health resources within this locale?
   b. If you were in need of mental health services, how would you proceed to seek help?
   c. What do you believe are some of the common emotional stressors impacting on individuals/families within your community?
   Have students report their findings and state implications for additional public education or mental health resources within the community.

Chapter 39
Psychosocial Home Care

Introduction

Home health care nursing, specifically psychosocial home health care nursing practice, is a service that strives to provide accessible and equitable care for individuals with long-term or enduring mental illness. Nurses are the major service providers of health care. They coordinate and manage home health care, which may include other disciplines, such as physical therapy, occupational therapy, and social work. The author discusses the six different ways through which home health care services can be provided.

The goals of psychosocial home care nursing are to prevent hospitalization and to provide the least restrictive alternative for treatment. It can help to relieve or resolve psychological and social problems facing clients and their families when they return home from inpatient and/or institutional care for a mental illness. Nurses involved in psychosocial home care may be generalists or specialists.

In order to explain psychosocial home care, the author discusses the three critical elements of historical underpinnings, philosophical foundations, and theoretical bases. Application of the nursing process to individuals requiring psychosocial home care is also described in detail. The psychosocial home care nurse is described as an individual who is confronted with many interpersonal and intrapersonal challenges and obstacles and who requires special treatment herself. Additionally, the whole practice of psychosocial home health care is both encouraged and limited by various legislative and political trends.

At the conclusion of Chapter 39, the author summarizes the following major points:

1. Home health care nursing and psychosocial home health care nursing are aspects of community health nursing and the community health movement.
2. Psychosocial home health care nursing is *not* an alternative to institutional care; the reverse is the case.
3. The goals of psychosocial home health care are to assist the client/family to gain or regain, maintain or restore, the optimum state of health and independence or to minimize and rehabilitate the effects of illness and disability either before or after institutionalization or to prevent institutionalization altogether.
4. The nursing process is used by the psychosocial home health care nurse to provide comprehensive services to clients in their places of residence.
5. Various social, legislative, and political forces make it likely that the need and demand for psychosocial home health care services will continue to increase.

Key Terms

Home health care nursing
Psychosocial home care nursing
Psychosocial clinical nurse specialist
Indirect care
Homebound

Teaching Strategies

1. Have students identify and visit the home health care service agencies in your area and seek out the following information:
   a. What type of agency are you? (Refer to "Providing Home Health Care," included in this chapter).
   b. Do you receive referrels for psychiatric patients/families? How many a month? Year? What is your referral source?
   c. What are the criteria that these patients/families must meet in order to be serviced by you?
   d. Which nurses are assigned to these patients/families? What are the nurses' titles? What is their educational preparation? What standards of practice do these nurses use in their care?
   e. What services do the nurses provide? How often? What is the cost to the patient/family?
   f. What are the most difficult challenges for the nurses working with this population? What are the satisfactions?
   g. Describe two or three psychosocial home care nursing cases that are open or have been open within the year. Include a review of the nursing care plan.
2. Have students write up a report of their visit (Teaching Strategy 1), discuss with the group, and write a letter describing their visit to one of the national associations or organizations concerned with home health care (see box in this chapter).

Chapter 40
Community Support and Rehabilitation

Introduction

Community support systems have been established in all areas of the country. They have made an amazing impact on the delivery system of broad-ranged services and supports needed by mentally ill individuals to live in the least restrictive environment while recognizing the need for quality of life. This chapter presents a historical and philosophical context for the development of community support systems, explores its impact on delivery systems to date, and projects trends that will continue to affect the delivery of community-based care. The 10 essential components defining a community support system are identified and described, as well as their goals. The author notes that access to a community support system is primarily through one of five models or their derivatives. Each model is described. Public policy and trends, which may act as obstacles and/or challenges to the delivery of care within community support systems, are highlighted and discussed in depth. Finally, the author describes, in detail, the knowledge and skills of nurses that make them uniquely prepared to assess, plan, intervene, and evaluate the following major points:

1. The National Institute of Mental Health has documented that local sites all over the nation are organizing community support systems and that states are mobilizing financial and legislative resources dedicated to the seriously and persistently mentally ill.

2. The research surrounding community support programs has demonstrated that when clients participate in community support programs: inpatient hospitalization is dropped by 50 percent; over a 1-year period, approximately two-thirds of clients show improvement or no deterioration; and there has been an increase in clients in community support programs from 4200 in 1980 to 350,000 in 1984.

3. Nurses have a leadership role in the development of a comprehensive community support service system that is committed to a holistic approach of intervening on both the client and the system level.

4. As we face the challenge of an easy answer (reinstitutionalization) versus the development of long-term social policy reforms that stimulate and support individuals in qualitative community alternatives, nursing must not only accept the challenge, but must remain in the forefront of these developments.

Key Terms

Community support program (CSP)
Community support system
Deinstitutionalization
Empowerment

Teaching Strategies

1. Have students identify which of the five access models is operational in your locale. Invite a representative of the model to your group. If possible, observe a caseworker during several hours of her day.
2. Have students discuss each of the public policy and trends noted in the chapter that create obstacles/challenges to the delivery of care within community support systems.
3. Have students speak to an individual, their parent(s), sibling, boss, etc. about the impact on their lives (before and after) community support program involvement.
4. Have students call the following individuals, asking them about their policies relative to hiring/renting to the chronically mentally ill:
   a. Department store manager
   b. Apartment complex manager
   c. McDonald's, Wendy's, Hardees, etc.
   d. Hospitals
   e. Others

Part Nine

Mental Health Interventions with the Medical Patient

Chapter 41
Trauma, Surgery, and Critical Care

Introduction

The stress experienced by the seriously ill patient is felt both by the client and by the entire family system. The stress is due to a combination of preexisting life stressors, stressors inherent to hospitalization, and injury- or illness-related stressors that interrupt the individual's and family's equilibrium. The seriously ill patient responds to these stressors both physiologically and psychologically. The author notes that the intensity and duration of the stress response depend on the patient's perception of the event, problem-solving skills, and conditioning factors.

In applying the nursing process to the critically ill person, the author states that the overall goal of nursing care is to return the patient to the highest possible level of physical and psychological functioning. The patient's response to injury or critical illness is explored through the phases of impact, resistance, and resolution. Specific patient responses for each phase are identified and discussed. Concurrent family responses to their critically ill member are examined, and suggestions for assessment are made.

This chapter applies the steps of the nursing process primarily to the psychosocial needs of the seriously ill patient and family. The author fully emphasizes that first priority must be given to the saving of lives, but she also realizes that because these needs will always be paramount, the psychological issues may need somewhat more attention. The outcome of psychological intervention often is not realized until long after the patient has left the critical care area.

Interventions involve three main areas for consideration: structuring the environment, sharing information, and providing emotional support. The author describes these interventions with special attention to the needs in each area of family members.

Complete evaluation of nursing intervention is often difficult because much of the patient's healing occurs outside of the critical care area. Nurses are encouraged to seek out patients and families who have been responded to.

The issue of "burnout" is one that particularly needs to be addressed by all who care for seriously ill patients. The author suggests primary prevention interventions for this group. Until this issue for these care-givers is addressed, serious problems that secondarily impact on patients' adaptation and growth will continue.

At the conclusion of Chapter 41, the author summarizes the following major points:

1. The assessment of the patient's response to trauma, surgery, or critical illness depends on his usual coping methods, problem-solving ability, and conditioning

factors such as available supports, previous health status, developmental level, and cultural background.

2. The response to trauma or serious illness varies from individual to individual, but generally follows a course of shock or impact, through resistance, and hopefully, to resolution.

3. Some of the emotional responses of patients to injury or critical illness include denial, body-image disturbances, feelings of loss of control, vulnerability, angry outbursts, and grief.

4. Family members of the critically ill patient also experience overwhelming anxiety, denial, anger, and rage.

5. Psychosocial interventions should be incorporated in the plan of care for the critically ill patient and his family, beginning with the patient's entrance into the hospital.

6. The focus of nursing intervention is the promotion of hope, control, trust, appropriate grieving, and reentry into the social world through sharing information, structuring the environment, and supporting the individual and family.

7. To provide optimal care to the injured or seriously ill, the nurse also needs to care for herself and accept peer support and recognition.

Key Terms

Hospital-related stressors
Illness-related stressors
Intensive care unit syndrome
Denial
Sensory overload

Impact
Resistance
Resolution
Framing memories
Divide time

Teaching Strategies

1. Have students spend at least 1 hour at the bedside of a critically ill person. Ask them to take note of the following and discuss later in supervision:
   a. The number of times the nursing staff made contact with the patient to specifically attend to psychological needs versus physical needs
   b. The number of verbal and nonverbal communications made to the patient of a psychosocial nature versus those of a physical care nature
   c. Therapeutic communication techniques most frequently observed; nontherapeutic communication techniques observed
   d. Remarks made by nurses to other staff members about the patient or the family but not intended to be heard by the patient
   e. Sensory stimuli or information made available or not available to the patient in assisting his orientation to time, place, and person
   f. Level of noise in the environment

2. Have students spend at least 1 hour, not in uniform, in the visiting room or area of a critical care unit. Have students take note of the following and discuss later in supervision:
   a. The number of times the family is interacted with by nurses, and for what purpose
   b. Concerns of family members verbalized

c. Feelings or coping mechanisms expressed by family behaviors
d. Examples of situations observed that could have been opportunities for helpful nursing interventions had a nurse been available
e. Comments made by family members, positive or negative, regarding nursing staff
f. Therapeutic or nontherapeutic techniques used by the nurses while interacting with family members—verbal and nonverbal examples

3. Have students plan *specific* activities to avoid the stress syndrome experienced by nurses working with seriously ill patients. Suggest that they use the author's encouragements related to self-awareness, peer groups, schedule changes, recreational interests, realistic goals, educational leaves, and taking and giving credit.

4. Have students discuss their thoughts and feelings relative to the ethical/moral issues of
   a. Allocation of scarce resources (*e.g.*, organ transplants)
   b. Whether or not to resuscitate a patient
   c. Life versus quality of life

5. Ask students to respond to the question, "Am I accountable to the patient, the institution, the physician, or myself?" when discussing ethical dilemmas.

6. Have students read and react to "It's over, Debbie," under Supportive Materials.

Supportive Materials

It's over, Debbie. JAMA 259:272, 1988

Lamb J, Rodgers D: Assisting the hostile, hospitalized child. Matern Child Nurs J 336–339, 1983

Righthand P: How to deal with rude, demanding, and unreasonable people. Nurs Life 28–32, 1983

Shubin S: Burnout: The professional hazard you face in nursing. Am J Nurs 78:22–27, 1978

Chapter 42
The Child at Risk: Illness, Hospitalization, and Disability

Introduction

Nonpsychiatric illness, disability, and hospitalization are crisis events for the child and family. Depending on the child and family's perception of the event, either positive or negative adaptation may occur. The nurse plays a key role in supporting the child and family toward growth and healthy adaptation.

In Chapter 42, the author explores the influences of hospitalization, parent-child attachment, and communication as factors that impact on the ill, disabled, or hospitalized child and the family as a unit. Knowledge of these influences, as well as awareness of one's own feelings and the impact that they can have, assist nurses in executing the nursing process in a manner that minimizes psychosocial distress for the child and family.

When assessing the child at risk because of illness, disability, or hospitalization, the nurse focuses attention on assessment of the child's *developmental level* with its concomitant needs, fears, and anxieties; on *environmental influences* such as the child's specific illness or disability, the child's previous life experiences, and the child's family; and on *personal idiosyncrasies* of the child. In addition, assessment of the psychosocial resources available in the particular health care setting to assist the child and family must be discerned.

The chapter emphasizes the pertinence of the concepts of trust, understanding, and mastery to delivering quality nursing care in the planning and intervention phases of the nursing process. By means of salient clinical examples with children of varied ages, the author illustrates nursing interventions based on these key concepts.

Evaluation strategies to examine the effectiveness of care are offered. Also, the author focuses on the need for nurses to engage in self-reflection about personal coping abilities and what resources are personally available and used while delivering care to the ill, disabled, or hospitalized child.

At the conclusion of Chapter 42, the author summarizes the following major points:

1. Long-lasting psychological disturbance has been found in 25 percent of pediatric hospital admissions.
2. Children with multiple admissions to the hospital in the first 4 years of life are the most vulnerable to psychological disturbance.
3. The influences of hospitalization, parent-child attachment, and communication are factors that the nurse recognizes and analyzes in applying the nursing process.
4. Assessment of the child at risk for psychosocial disturbance in health care includes gathering information about the child's developmental level, the environmental

influences on the child, such as the nature of the specific illness or disability, the child's previous life experiences, the child's family, and personal attributes of the child.

5. Planning and interventions for the child who is ill, disabled, or hospitalized are evaluated for effectiveness in supporting the child's and family's development of trust, understanding, and mastery of the stresses involved in health care.

6. Preparation for experiences encountered in health care and the use of play are common, yet critical, psychosocial interventions.

7. Mastery allows the child to be active on his own behalf, to turn from a passive victim to a participating role.

8. Interventions to support mastery are those that allow the child active exploration of feelings, as in nondirective play and expressive arts; that enhance the child's and family's self-concept and self-esteem; and promote family-centered care.

9. Evaluation of the effectiveness of nursing intervention is based on observation and analysis of the child's and family's behavior and self-reflection.

10. The nurse's acceptance of the advocacy role, coupled with the responsibility to minimize potential psychological disturbances and to maximize growth potentials, affords the challenges and rewards of the nursing of children.

Key Terms

Adaptation
Resilience
Rooming-in
Mastery
Intellectualization
Identification

Denial
Idiosyncratic rituals
Medical play
Stress immunization
Thought-stopping
Relaxation training

Teaching Strategies

1. Have students visit the Child Life–Child Development Department (play therapy department) and observe what toys, books, and activities are available within the department. Have students discuss with the departmental personnel how and why the choices were made to have those particular items available. Have students report how the particular items relate to the concepts of trust, understanding, and mastery that were presented in Chapter 42. This type of exercise also could be expanded to include the students' assessment of other psychosocial resources that were described in the chapter.

2. Have students discuss the differences and similarities in their thoughts and feelings when delivering care to a chronically ill or disabled child versus when delivering care to a chronically ill or disabled adult. Does the age of the person impact on the reaction? If so, why? If not, why not? As they think about their personal reactions, what issues or experiences from their own past seem to be connected with the thoughts and feelings generated in the present?

3. Have students discuss the relationship between the common fears and anxieties of children in health care outlined in Chapter 42 and the phase-specific developmental needs and tasks of infancy through adolescence. (Referral to Chapter 18 of the text may be useful.) Have them propose specific nursing interventions, based on

theoretical rationale, which would assist the child in each developmental phase to minimize fear and anxiety during hospitalization.

4. Require that students integrate attention to the psychosocial needs of the child and family into their care of the nonpsychiatrically ill, disabled, or hospitalized child. Have students use the outline for assessment given in Chapter 42. For the remaining phases of the nursing process, have them be accountable for planning, delivering, and describing care that aims, as the chapter's author states:
    a. To minimize the potential for psychosocial disturbance in the child as the state of physical health is being restored or supported
    b. To maximize the opportunities for psychosocial benefit to the child as the state of physical well-being is restored or supported
    c. To provide assistance to the child's development of trust, understanding, and mastery of the stressful experiences in health care
    d. To respond to the child as an individual with unique needs

5. Have students visit support groups that are available to parents of children with chronic illnesses. Examples of groups may include Heart to Heart (an organization for families of children with heart disorders) and the Candlelighters (an organization for families of children with cancer). Have the students assess the psychosocial needs communicated by parents in these meetings and discuss how they believe that the data could impact on their nursing role when caring for the child and family.

Supportive Materials

Bernardo ML: Conceptual model of children's cognitive adaptation to physical disability. J Adv Nurs 7:595–601, 1982

Dorn LD: Children's concepts of illness: Clinical applications. Pediatr Nurs 325–327, 1984

Lyon J: Playing God in the Nursery. New York, WW Norton, 1985

Nagera H: Children's reactions to hospitalization and illness. Child Psychiatry Hum Dev 9:3–19, 1978

Chapter 43
Issues in Women's Health Care

Introduction

Since women are the largest group of consumers of health care today, the author suggests that nurses need to be competent and sensitive to the health care issues important to women and should be interested in the meaning these issues have for women. Because of the ever-changing role of women in today's society, females are extremely susceptible to stress and distress, which can lead to disease. The newer roles of women emerging in today's society have many consequences for their mental health. The author reminds the nurse of her responsibility to help women cope with conflict, change, and stress.

In discussing the politics of women's health care, the author focuses on the significant attitudes that seemed to have emerged historically. Such patriarchal beliefs as the inferior and dependent nature of women are major obstacles to women in procuring appropriate health care responses to their special needs. In order to assist women with such issues, the nurse-leader is reminded of the need to plan and implement strategies that assist women to become more independent and powerful in matters of their own health care.

The author describes and discusses the concepts of self-image, loss, anxiety, stress, and powerlessness as they relate to women in health care. Additionally, the significant events in the life of a woman, childbearing and parenting, hysterectomy and mastectomy, and menopause, are studied in depth by way of the nursing process. Psychosocial assessment tools are suggested and included within the discussion of each event. The Roy adaptation framework is highlighted and suggested by the author throughout this section.

At the conclusion of Chapter 43, the author summarizes the following major points:

1. Today's female seeking health care faces conflicts related to the traditional and emerging roles of women in our society.
2. Women's traditional place within the health care system has been a subordinate one, but that is presently being questioned.
3. Many of women's health problems are related to how the person perceives her physical and personal selves.
4. The nurse frequently deals with the recurring themes of loss, anxiety, stress, and powerlessness in the health care of women.
5. Application of the nursing process to the specific issues of childbearing and parenting, the surgical alterations of hysterectomy and mastectomy, and the menopause includes consideration of the psychosocial significance of these events.
6. Psychosocial assessment of the woman client in the health care setting is based on the Roy adaptation framework, addressing the client's self-concept, role, and interrelationships.
7. General interventions to promote adaptation to these common health alterations

include therapeutic communication, mutual goal setting, health care teaching, and anticipatory guidance.

8. By designing nursing care to meet the needs of the whole person, nurses can have a significant impact on the woman client experiencing childbearing and parenting, surgical alterations , or menopause, as well as other issues in women's health care.

Key Terms

Liberal feminists
Radical feminists
Marxist feminists
Self concept:
    Body image
    Personal self

Loss
Anxiety
Powerlessness
Grief process
Reach for Recovery
Encore

Teaching Strategies

1. Have students read a copy of *McCall's*, *Good Housekeeping*, *Cosmopolitan*, *Seventeen*, or *Playgirl* in order to make observations about the mixture of women in today's society. Have students discuss their observations in general and specifically related to the health care needs and interests of women today. Have them also discuss their thoughts about the lack of a singular, solidifying philosophy and view of today's woman and the impact this may have on the health care resources available to women.

2. Have students imagine that within the next 3 days they will deliver a healthy baby of their own. Discuss the following questions:
   a. In what way would you handle the restrictions of being tied down? What resources are or are not available in your community to assist you?
   b. How would the nightly sleep interruptions affect your level of functioning, level of anxiety/stress, and self-concept? What resources are or are not available to you to assist you?
   c. How would you handle or not handle the general housekeeping and living chores necessary? What choices would you make? How would you feel about having to make these choices?
   d. How would you handle your fatigue? What resources are or are not available to you?
   e. What impact might this child have on your relationship with your spouse? Boyfriend? Family? Friends?
   f. How might your responses to questions a. through e. influence your current health status? Future health status? What resources are or are not available to you for health care?

3. Repeat exercise 2 assuming that you are one of the following. Discuss the differences and problems facing women today.
   a. A 15-year-old unmarried mother living at home with a working parent
   b. A 32-year-old employed secretary and single parent of a 7- and 10-year-old
   c. A middle-class, married, nonworking 27-year-old mother of a 4-year-old
   d. A 38-year-old married and employed first-time mother who makes $35,000 a year

4. Using the tools suggested in the chapter, have students assess a patient in an obstetrics and gynecology clinic. After presenting their assessment to the group, have the students identify actual and potential problems in adaptation, with suggestions for goals and interventions. (Student focus should be directed to a prenatal patient, a recent mastectomy or hysterectomy patient, or a patient visiting a clinic with primary or secondary problems related to menopause.)
5. Have students discuss the list of myths and misconceptions about menopause noted in the chapter. For each myth, have the students discuss the *facts* that are contrary to the myth.
6. Have students contact Reach for Recovery through the American Cancer Society and either talk to the volunteers about their services or visit a patient with a volunteer.

Supportive Materials

Taylor C: Women's issues in psychiatric nursing. In Lego S (ed): The American Handbook of Psychiatric Nursing, pp 601–607. Philadelphia, JB Lippincott, 1984

Chapter 44
Death and Dying

Introduction

No living organism is exempt from experiencing the inevitable event of death. Chapter 44 examines the meaning of death and dying, as well as common reactions to these experiences, from a broad theoretical, philosophical, religious, and "American" perspective. Moving from the broad to a more specific focus, the author examines what death really means to clients, their family and friends, and the health care professionals caring for them.

Many tangible and intangible variables impact on the meaning that the client attaches to the experience of death and dying. For example, transferring the dying client from the privacy of home to the depersonalized setting of an institution can engender varied intense feelings of isolation and loneliness for the client. Also, when dying clients are saddled with the expectations that accompany the sick role, as well as the stigma of approaching nonexistence, they experience a myriad of feelings associated with loss.

For family members and friends of the dying client, the experience is often more difficult than for the one who is dying. Engaging in the anticipatory grief work while the loved one is dying can be extremely helpful as the survivors prepare for the ultimate separation and loss that accompany death and as they actually experience the process of mourning after the loss occurs. In Chapter 44, the author also examines common behavioral responses and feelings associated with various stages of the grief process.

Working with clients who are dying triggers many reactions in health care professionals. Symbolically, death and dying may threaten the professional's aim to promote health and life. In addition, professionals are confronted with the awareness that someday they too will die. To be truly effective in caring for the dying person, professionals must come to terms with their own ultimate death and the meaning that they personally attach to death.

Chapter 44 also examines various theories of death and dying, including the levels of awareness of dying as proposed by Glaser and Strauss and the stages of dying described by Kübler-Ross. In addition, reactions of survivors to sudden unexpected death and to the death of a child are discussed.

Physical and psychological nursing care of the dying patient and family is highlighted in the latter section of the chapter. The delivery of positive quality physical care can offer much comfort and reassurance to the dying person and family and is frequently a priority item. Psychological care aims to respond to the unique needs and goals of the patient and family. The author suggests that the quality of psychological care received by the patient and family will be enhanced if the nurse incorporates the following guidelines into the care delivered: Provide information to patients and family, assist patients to maintain autonomy or assure patients that they will not be abandoned (assuring safe conduct), support patients in experiencing meaningfulness, and promote an appropriate death for patients.

At the conclusion of Chapter 44, the author summarizes the following major points:

1. Contemporary reactions to death involve avoidance and preoccupation with death as a destructive force.
2. Advances in medical practice have altered the nature and location of treatment of the dying.
3. The dying client faces the fear of abandonment, initiation into the "sick role," and stigmatization, all of which further isolate him.
4. Family and friends of the dying experience feelings of loss and anticipatory grief to prepare for the death of their loved one.
5. As a result of the grieving process, the survivors free themselves from the bonds of the deceased, reorient themselves to their environment from which the deceased is absent, and establish new relationships.
6. Working with the dying elicits both a personal and a professional threat in health care providers.
7. Kübler-Ross identified five stages of dying experienced by the patient and his family—denial, anger, bargaining, depression, and acceptance.
8. Sudden, unexpected death allows no time for the survivors to engage in anticipatory grief.
9. Competent physical nursing care of the dying patient reassures the family and significant others and adds to their emotional well-being.
10. Psychological nursing care of the dying is based on the patient's and family's goals and needs and incorporates the provision of information, autonomy, safe conduct, meaningfulness, and appropriate death.

Key Terms

Anticipatory grief
Stages of mourning:
    Impact
    Middle stage
    Accommodation
Grief work

Stages of dying:
    Denial
    Anger
    Bargaining
    Depression
    Acceptance
    Disengagement

Teaching Strategies

1. Have students complete unfinished sentences such as the following:
   a. If I were told today that I had 3 months to live, I would feel _____
   _____.
   b. If I were told today that I had 3 months to live, I would tell _____
   because _____.
   c. If I were told today that I had 3 months to live, how I structure my daily time
   would _____
   _____.
   d. When I think of death, I _____
   _____.
   e. The death of _____
   was (would be) the hardest for me because _____.

f. The most difficult thing for me in working with a dying patient and family would be _____
_____.

g. The easiest thing for me in working with a dying patient and family would be _____
_____.

2. Have students write a paper that focuses on their own death. Ask them to address objectives such as the following:
   a. Describe fantasies about your own dying process (how old will you be, what will you die of, and so on).
   b. Describe your relationship with significant others during the process of your dying (who will be important to you, in what way, and why?).
   c. Describe the greatest fears that you will experience.
   d. Describe the sources of your greatest comfort.
   e. Relate how you would like your obituary to read.

3. Have students role-play interactions between nurse and dying patient, nurse and family member of a dying patient, nurse and friend of a dying patient, nurse and nurse whose patient recently died. Then have students discuss the following:
   a. Thoughts and feelings generated during the experience
   b. Similarities and differences between the nurse's communication with the dying patient, the family member, the friend, and the nurse peer
   c. Projected similarities and differences between the nurse's communication with the above named persons and a person who is psychiatrically ill

4. Have students read and discuss the living will included in Chapter 44. What are their beliefs about having the right to self-determination? How would they respond as a professional to a dying person who has made a living will?

5. Have students delineate specific nursing interventions related to the psychological factors of care (*i.e.*, information, autonomy, safe conduct, meaningfulness, appropriate death) presented in Chapter 44.

Supportive Materials

Barry PD: Psychological Nursing Assessment and Intervention, pp 255–278. Philadelphia, JB Lippincott, 1984

Part Ten

Professional Issues in Psychiatric-Mental Health Nursing

Chapter 45
Legal Implications of Psychiatric-Mental Health Nursing

Introduction

Psychiatric nurses, possibly more than any other group of nurses, must practice in such a way that they meet their professional standards of practice. Moreover, they must share a vested interest in policing those standards to the extent that the standards remain in compliance with the local, state, and national legal standards. The major goal of this chapter is stated as preparing nurses to include legal principles in their psychiatric-mental health nursing practice both to benefit and protect the nurse and to enhance the quality of care that the patient receives.

The author begins by defining both nursing practice and malpractice. The time has now come when the nurse is often a co-defendant in a malpractice suit along with the physician and the hospital. All psychiatric nurses are responsible and accountable for certain acts of omission and commission. Areas of responsibility include informed consent, confidentiality, and providing legally acceptable nursing care. Throughout this chapter, the author repeatedly assigns the nurse to the patient advocate role. Therefore, a full understanding of the legal rights of patients is incumbent on the practicing psychiatric-mental health nurse.

Legal issues of special patient populations are described. Persons who have been charged with crimes may be hospitalized for a determination of their ability to stand trial or an evaluation of the defendant's mental condition at the time of the crime. Juveniles also may be admitted to psychiatric facilities, but now neutral fact finders must determine whether legal requirements for admission exist in addition to parental authorization.

The author discusses many of the newer and evolving legal rights of patients that have been won through major court cases. *Wyatt v. Stickney* focused specifically on the right to treatment. *Covington v. Harris* held that persons who are to be treated involuntarily should receive the treatment in a setting that is the least restrictive to their liberty.

Finally, this chapter discusses and describes the major strategies for ensuring quality and accountability in nursing practice. The American Nurses' Association (ANA) Standards of Practice assist in determining clinical standards for generic and specialty areas of practice. Quality assurance programs such as audits and peer reviews exist in institutions to constantly evaluate nursing practice. Some agencies use a legal consultation and educational program as a quality assurance strategy.

At the conclusion of Chapter 45, the author summarizes the following major points:

1. Nurses have both independent and dependent areas of nursing practice and are liable for maintenance of a responsible standard of care to clients in both of these areas of practice.

2. A failure to meet the standard of care that results in an injury to a client-consumer makes the nurse liable for nursing negligence or malpractice.

3. Nurses have a duty to participate in the issues of informed consent, which are a basic right of clients; failure to obtain informed consent from a client prior to a procedure can result in a civil action against the physician and the health care agency on the theories of assault and battery or malpractice.

4. Clients also have a right to rely on the appropriateness and confidentiality of their medical records and data.

5. Confidentiality is an ethical, professional, and legal responsibility and is, in many instances, mandated by statute.

6. Privileged communication is determined by statute for certain professional groups and their clients.

7. Some cases indicate that confidentiality must be breached when the public safety is in jeopardy, as when clients threaten to harm third persons.

8. To provide legally acceptable nursing care in psychiatric-mental health settings, nurses must be informed about a variety of issues, including recognized client rights, and they must take responsibility with other health team members to see that client rights are protected.

9. Client rights may differ due to the civil or criminal nature of commitment proceedings, the voluntariness of a civil commitment, the purpose of the criminal commitment, and the age of the client.

10. It is most important that psychiatric-mental health care-givers identify client status and client rights and secure adequate consultation as client rights evolve.

11. Three strategies for enhancing the quality of psychiatric-mental health nursing care and, thereby, ensuring quality care and accountability by nursing to consumers are as follows:
    a. Nurses must practice by using ANA Standards of Practice as their normative base.
    b. Nurses must develop, and participate in, quality assurance programming, including psychiatric audit.
    c. Nurses must request and secure ongoing continuing education and consultation with an attorney who is knowledgeable in mental health law.

Key Terms

Malpractice
Reasonable man test
Battery
Respondent superior
Informed consent
Substituted consent
Voluntary admission
Emergency involuntary admission

Indefinite involuntary admission
Forensic psychiatry
Competency to stand trial
McNaughten rule
Mens rea

Teaching Strategies

1. Have students make a list and define all key terms in this chapter and use this terminology during discussions of this chapter. Add the following terms to their

list: *assault, tort, dependent* and *independent functions* of the nurse, and *negligence*.

2. Have students compare and contrast the nurse practice act in their state with one in a state very different from their own in terms of geographic location, size, and so on. Discuss the strengths and weaknesses.

3. Invite a lawyer to supervise the discussion of examples of both successful and unsuccessful negligence suits against nurses. Have the students apply the five elements of nursing negligence discussed in this chapter in order to guess the outcomes of the cases presented. (This exercise may be done without a lawyer present.) Additionally, discuss the "Case Study—Practice or Malpractice?" included in this chapter.

4. Have students examine any and all consent forms used by the psychiatric-mental health agencies with whom you are involved. Ask students to query nursing staff regarding their knowledge and understanding of the nurse's role in obtaining a patient signature on a consent form.

5. Have students review this chapter, making a list of the rights of psychiatric patients. Have them categorize the list using the following format:

Psychiatric Patient Rights					
All Patients		Voluntary Patients		Involuntary Patients	
Lose	Retain	Lose	Retain	Lose	Retain

6. Have students investigate the judicial commitment legislation in your state. Have students request permission to observe a commitment or a committeeship proceeding. Discuss thoughts, feelings, and observations as a group. (Refer to the two case studies about commitment in this chapter.)

7. Have students discuss their role as patient advocate in a psychiatric-mental health setting. Ask them to identify specific nursing behaviors, with examples, that would demonstrate their advocacy.

8. Have students attend community support groups such as Friends and Family of the Mentally Ill or the Association of the Mentally Ill to identify patient and family legal concerns and efforts to develop, amend, or strike down legislation governing the care and treatment of the mentally ill. Discuss in supervision.

Supportive Materials

Alexis A: Body searches and the right to privacy. JPNMHS 24:21–25, 1986

Creighton H: Law Every Nurse Should Know. Philadelphia, WB Saunders, 1981

Oriol M, Oriol R: Involuntary commitment and the right to refuse medication. JPNMHS 24:15–20, 1986

Sanders J, Du Plessis D: An historical view of right to treatment. JPNMHS 23:12–17, 1985

Snyder M: Legal issues in psychiatric nursing. In Lego S (ed): The American Handbook of Psychiatric Nursing, pp 593–600. Philadelphia, JB Lippincott, 1984

Chapter 46
Research in Psychiatric-Mental Health Nursing

Introduction

Conducting research (gathering and processing information) has been a significant component of nursing for a lengthy period of time. The author of Chapter 46 illuminates this thought as she presents the definition and purpose of research and an overview of the research process, with emphasis on how the scientific method can be and is applied in nursing situations.

Special emphasis is given to the need for nurses to use research in their practice. In an effort to assist nurses with accomplishing this goal, the author elaborates on four areas of published research reports that require nurses' attention and critique: introduction, methodology, results, and discussion.

In addition to discussing the safeguards inherent in using the scientific method when conducting research, the author emphasizes the ethics that guide the nurse in protecting subjects' rights. First, the nurse must respect the fact that refusal to participate in any research project is a person's right. Coercion or the denial of a person's choice to refuse participation is absolutely unethical. Second, all potential research subjects have the right to informed consent. This means that the nurse must fully inform the potential research subject about what participation in the project means, what the potential implications are, what time commitment would be required, and what risk factors are possible. Last, all subjects have the right to confidentiality.

In the final sections of the chapter, the author speaks candidly to the student and encourages and promotes participation in nursing research. She delineates specific steps and guides that can assist students in responding to the challenge of reading, evaluating, and using information gleaned from research studies in their practice and ultimately taking the risk to become an active participant in the conduct of nursing research and adding to nursing knowledge.

At the conclusion of Chapter 46, the author summarizes the following major points:

1. The research process can be applied by any professionals interested in obtaining data or information.
2. The safeguards of the steps of the research process provide structure and consistency to information gathering.
3. Research reports contain four areas:
   a. The introduction describing the problem investigated and related background information

b. The methodology describing the population and sample, research instruments, and procedures for data collection and data analysis

c. The results of the report, describing the analysis and interpretation of the data

d. The discussion describing the conclusions drawn from the study and the implications of the findings in relation to nursing practice

4. The individual subject possesses the right to refuse to participate in the research, the right to informed consent, and the right to confidentiality.

5. The expanding role of nurses today includes participation in nursing research and the application of research results to nursing practice.

Key Terms

Research
Nursing research
Research types (approaches)
Components of the research report:
    Introduction
    Methodology
        Population
        Sample
        Research instrument
            Reliability
            Validity
                Face validity
                Content validity
                Construct validity
                Criterion-related validity
        Data collection
        Data analysis
            Descriptive statistics
            Inferential statistics
    Results
    Discussion
Protection of subjects' rights:
    Refusal to participate
    Informed consent
    Confidentiality
        Anonymity

Teaching Strategies

1. Have students in clinical conferences or class identify problems or questions that are significant to them. Encourage this activity frequently during their psychiatric-mental health experiences, as well as throughout their entire curriculum.

2. As the author of Chapter 46 states, "The best introduction to the realm of research is to read about it." Assign at least one research article as a required reading for each content area presented during this course. Address the article during lecture and encourage student discussion. (Many of the references cited at the end of each

chapter include research articles.)

3. Encourage students to develop research critiquing skills. Assign students, either individually or as a small group, to critique a published research study that you assign. Have students use the critique methodology proposed by the author of Chapter 46 or one that you develop.

4. Share with students the existing protocol at your institution for the conduct of human research. Also, share examples of protection of subjects' rights (informed consent) forms. Have them critique these data for ethical safeguards of subjects.

Chapter 47
Trends in Psychiatric-Mental Health Care

Introduction

The available psychiatric-mental health services in our society and the numerous roles of the psychiatric-mental health nurse in providing case have evolved to their current status in response to numerous challenges to and advances in the field of psychiatric-mental health. Chapter 47 examines current challenges facing the field and the concomitant demand for responses that reflect an understanding of the reality orientation of the challenges.

Challenges that cannot be ignored by psychiatric-mental health nurses emanate from the arena of society at large, economics and legislation, technology, and the health care system. For example, compared with even 25 years ago, society currently demonstrates a considerably increased focus on the needs and rights of various sectors of the population, including the elderly, the family, women, and certain minority groups. Also, changes in the economy have spurred a dramatic decrease in external funding to mental health service, education, and research and have added increased stress especially to those who are unemployed. Similarly, a myriad of technological advances such as computers and electronic media (television, videotapes) tremendously affect the relationship between mental health providers and society at large. In addition, the health care system itself evidences rapid growth shifts in biologic as well as psychological health care delivery.

This whirlwind of change must be responded to by psychiatric-mental health nurses. Directions for accountably and responsibly responding to the changes emanate from within the profession of nursing. The author discusses four pertinent American Nurses' Association documents that serve as prime resources to assist psychiatric-mental health nurses in their active response to persons living in a constantly changing environment. These resources include the following:

1. *The Statement on Psychiatric and Mental Health Nursing Practice* (1967, revised 1976)
2. *The Standards of Practice of Psychiatric and Mental Health Nursing Practice* (1973, revised 1982)
3. *The Code for Nurses with Interpretive Statements* (1976)
4. *Nursing: A Social Policy Statement* (1980)

The author suggests that psychiatric-mental health nurses' responses to the changes can be evaluated by examining four key areas of change—changes in care providers, changes in roles in practice settings, changes in the activity of psychiatric-mental health nurses, and changes in the focus of care. For each key area of change addressed, pertinent specific examples of nursing activity are included. For example, significant advances have been made in the educational preparation and opportunities available for psychiatric-mental health nurses. In addition, considerable contribution to health care delivery is made by psychiatric-mental health nurses in various roles such as staff nurse, clinical nurse specialist, liaison, consultant, administrator, and psychotherapist.

At the conclusion of Chapter 47, the author summarizes the following major points:

1. Nursing's response to the challenges of mental health care has been to provide a variety of practitioners who are capable of serving clients in an inpatient or community setting.
2. Another significant nursing response to this challenge is to integrate psychiatric-mental health nursing concepts into the generic preparation of all nurses.
3. Psychiatric-mental health nurses assume leadership and practice roles in all types of health care delivery systems.
4. Presently, the most significant threat to the psychiatric-mental health nursing practice is one shared by all mental health practitioners—economic destruction.
5. Despite economic disasters and the high costs of service, mental health professionals must not lose their awareness of the pain and suffering caused by mental disorders, and they must use the available political, social, and professional avenues to alleviate that suffering.
6. The demand for skill in mental health consultation will increase.
7. The need for psychiatric nurses who specialize in the care of the chronically mentally disturbed and mentally disturbed youths will continue to outdistance the number of nurses prepared in these areas.
8. Psychiatric-mental health nurses will develop new funding sources to maintain and promote the graduate educational programs necessary to carry out nursing research.

Key Terms

The statement on psychiatric and mental health nursing
The standards of practice of psychiatric mental health nursing
The code of nurses with interpretive statements
Nursing: A social policy statement
Roles of psychiatric-mental health nurses:
    Staff nurse
    Clinical nurse specialist
    Psychiatric nurse liaison
    Nurse as Psychotherapist
    Nurse leader

Teaching Strategies

1. Have four small groups of students prepare and deliver a presentation that focuses on the four American Nurses' Association documents discussed in Chapter 47. The presentation may relate to issues such as the following:
   a. Purpose of the document
   b. Major points made in the document
   c. Variables that did or may have influenced the association's preparation of the document
   d. Ways in which nurses do and could use the document to enhance delivery of nursing care in general and psychiatric-mental health nursing care specifically

2. Invite as guest lecturers a panel of psychiatric-mental health nurses representing the roles described in Chapter 47. Have them share with students information such as the following:
   a. What impacted on their choice to enter psychiatric nursing?
   b. The duties and responsibilities associated with their present position.
   c. How they view psychiatric-mental health nursing responding to the challenges delineated in Chapter 47.
   d. Future needs of mental health care from their perspective.
3. Have students write a paper entitled "Psychiatric-Mental Health Nursing: The Year 2025." Have students address their projection of how societal changes will present challenges to the psychiatric-mental health care field and how nursing will respond to these challenges.
4. Have students seek out and discuss the curriculum and terminal objectives of any master's and/or doctoral programs offering a psychiatric-mental health specialty or subspecialty.
5. Have students investigate and attend a meeting of their local association of the Alliance for the Mentally Ill.